Traveling through Video Games

This book unlocks an understanding of video games as virtual travel. It explains how video game design increasingly takes cues from the promotional language of tourism, and how this connection raises issues of power and commodification.

Bridging the disciplinary gap between game and tourism studies, the book offers a comprehensive account of touristic gazing in games such as *The Legend of Zelda: Breath of the Wild*, *Minecraft*, and *Microsoft Flight Simulator 2020*. Traveling through video games involves a mythological promise of open-ended opportunity, summarized in the slogan *you can go there*. Van Nuenen discusses the scale of game worlds, the elusive nature of freedom and control, and the pivotal role of work in creating a sense of belonging. The logic of tourism is fundamentally consumptive—but through design choices, players can also be invited to approach their travels more critically. This is the difference between moving through a game world, and *being moved* by it.

This interdisciplinary and innovative study will interest students and scholars of digital media studies, game studies, tourism and technology, and the Digital Humanities.

Tom van Nuenen is a researcher and educator in data science and algorithmic culture. He works as a Lecturer and Assistant Project Scientist at the University of California at Berkeley, USA.

Routledge Advances in Game Studies

Forms and Functions of Endings in Narrative Digital Games
Michelle Herte

Independent Videogames
Cultures, Networks, Techniques and Politics
Edited by Paolo Ruffino

Comics and Videogames
From Hybrid Medialities to Transmedia Expansions
Edited by Edited by Andreas Rauscher, Daniel Stein, and Jan-Noël Thon

Immersion, Narrative, and Gender Crisis in Survival Horror Video Games
Andrei Nae

Videogames and the Gothic
Ewan Kirkland

Longing, Ruin, and Connection in Hideo Kojima's Death Stranding
Amy M. Green

Manifestations of Queerness in Video Games
Gaspard Pelurson

Representing Conflicts in Games
Antagonism, Rivalry, and Competition
Edited by Björn Sjöblom, Jonas Linderoth, and Anders Frank

Videogames and Agency
Bettina Bódi

Posthuman Gaming
Avatars, Gamers, and Entangled Subjectivities
Poppy Wilde

Traveling through Video Games
Tom van Nuenen

Traveling through Video Games

Tom van Nuenen

LONDON AND NEW YORK

First published 2024
by Routledge
4 Park Square, Milton Park, Abingdon, Oxon OX14 4RN

and by Routledge
605 Third Avenue, New York, NY 10158

Routledge is an imprint of the Taylor & Francis Group, an informa business

© 2024 Tom van Nuenen

The right of Tom van Nuenen to be identified as author of this work has been asserted in accordance with sections 77 and 78 of the Copyright, Designs and Patents Act 1988.

All rights reserved. No part of this book may be reprinted or reproduced or utilised in any form or by any electronic, mechanical, or other means, now known or hereafter invented, including photocopying and recording, or in any information storage or retrieval system, without permission in writing from the publishers.

Trademark notice: Product or corporate names may be trademarks or registered trademarks, and are used only for identification and explanation without intent to infringe.

British Library Cataloguing-in-Publication Data
A catalogue record for this book is available from the British Library

Library of Congress Cataloging-in-Publication Data
Names: Van Nuenen, Tom, 1984- author.
Title: Traveling through video games / by Tom van Nuenen.
Description: New York : Routledge, 2024. | Series: Routledge advances in game studies | Includes bibliographical references and index. |
Identifiers: LCCN 2023036221 (print) | LCCN 2023036222 (ebook) | ISBN 9781032519487 (hbk) | ISBN 9781032519500 (pbk) | ISBN 9781003404590 (ebk)
Subjects: LCSH: Video games--Social aspects. | Tourism--Computer network resources. | Virtual reality.
Classification: LCC GV1469.34.S52 V36 2024 (print) | LCC GV1469.34.S52 (ebook) | DDC 794.8--dc23/eng/20230828
LC record available at https://lccn.loc.gov/2023036221
LC ebook record available at https://lccn.loc.gov/2023036222

ISBN: 978-1-032-51948-7 (hbk)
ISBN: 978-1-032-51950-0 (pbk)
ISBN: 978-1-003-40459-0 (ebk)

DOI: 10.4324/9781003404590

Typeset in Times New Roman
by Deanta Global Publishing Services, Chennai, India

Contents

Acknowledgments   vii

1 Introduction   1

Why This Book 5
Notes 9
References 10

2 It's All Under Control   13

Pixels and Passports 16
The Issue with Flow 19
An Unsettling Vacation 21
Defamiliarizing Play 23
Notes 27
References 28

3 King of the Sandbox   31

Gamified History 31
Hiding From the City, In the City 36
It's All in the Details 40
A Meaningless Overview 45
Notes 47
References 48

4 Bigger on the Inside   51

Touring the Walking Sim 52
Going Off Script 57
Resignation and Subversion 60
Walking in Space Boots 62
Notes 66
References 66

5	**You Can Stay Here**	70

Scale Matters 71
Relaxing Survival 75
Life's a Chore 78
Notes 83
References 84

6	**When Here Becomes There**	87

Pedestrian Gamification 87
Racing Through Utopia 90
Keep it Professional 93
Elective Alienation 95
It's All in Your Mind 99
Notes 100
References 100

7	**Conclusion**	102

Key Themes 103
Notes 105
References 105

Index   *107*

Acknowledgments

My Ph.D. supervisor once suggested I split a paper in two because I had too much material. This work is the result of a similar method. My book *Scripted Journeys*, on tourism and algorithmic technology, included a chapter on video games: it quickly became too bloated for its own good. It turns out the connections between tourism and games are both rich and understudied. I hope this book can play a small part in initiating a more thorough conversation.

Throughout the years, several people have helped me flesh out and reflect on the ideas expressed here: in particular Jelle Goossens, Inge van de Ven, Odile Heynders, Marlijn van Nuenen, Ava Carl, and Espen Aarseth. I also want to thank several people for their generous comments on various parts of this work: Barry Horwitz, Geoffrey Long, Julia Genster, and the anonymous reviewers at Routledge. Finally, I want to give special thanks to Hillary Voigt for helping me navigate this book across the finish line.

Tom van Nuenen
Berkeley
September 2023

1 Introduction

The story goes that in the late 1950s, seven-year-old Shigeru Miyamoto started exploring the bamboo forests and limestone caves outside his home in the countryside of Sonobe. His small village lies on the Sea of Japan, about thirty miles from Kyoto. On one of his trips, he found a hole in the ground. The next day he returned with a lantern and crawled in.

The sense of awe and excitement Miyamoto felt allegedly inspired him to design the 1986 video game *The Legend of Zelda*,[1] the first entry in one of the most popular franchises in the medium's history. The game's story involves a familiar template for young adult fiction: a boy named Link is called by a divine entity to save the land of Hyrule and its princess. However, upon starting the game, the only thing that stands out is a cave, represented by a basic black square, where you will find a sword. Entering the cave is entirely optional: players can choose to walk in a cardinal direction to begin exploring the game's world. But that black square is such an obvious cue that very few players will have skipped it.

Tellingly, what Miyamoto found in his childhood cave has never been part of the story. That black square stands for the unknown, the potential of adventure that games would be searching to fulfill for decades to come. In that context, the cave serves mostly as punctuation to that which houses it: an open world waiting to be explored.

What set Zelda apart from other action-adventure games of its era, such as *Berzerk*[2] or the Ultima series,[3] was the ambiance of its environment. The game's top-down perspective was made to resemble a diorama—or, as Miyamoto himself called it, a "miniature garden" that you can put into a drawer and visit anytime you like.[4] From the Romantic poets of Europe to the Zen gardens of Japan, the garden has symbolized harmony and safety. But that is not what drew Miyamoto's players in. It was curiosity and the thrill of a potential adventure: the sense that there must be something in that cave, waiting to be seen.

Over the years, the drawer of Miyamoto's miniature garden became harder to shut. In 1998, *N64 Magazine* wrote their glowing review of *The Legend of Zelda: Ocarina of Time* (*OOT*),[5] the first three-dimensional game in the series. The boundaries had shifted: the camera was now positioned behind Link, and

DOI: 10.4324/9781003404590-1

2 Introduction

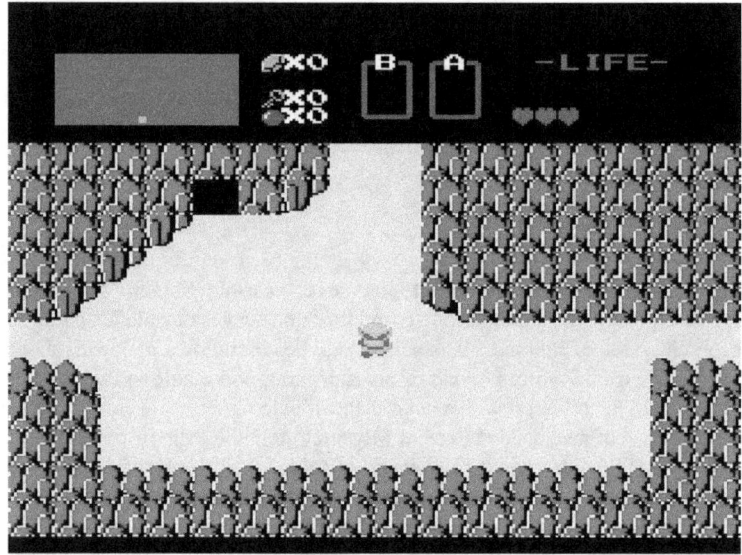

Figure 1.1 The Legend of Zelda opening screen. Author screenshot.

players could look over his shoulders and into the distance. The review took the tone of a tourist brochure: "There's Hyrule Castle looming large in the distance and Lon Lon Ranch off to your left, but from now on you can pretty much go wherever you want."[6] On the next page of the magazine, we see a picture of Link standing in a graveyard, captioned: "Just look how far you can see into the distance"[7] (see Figure 1.2).

Looking back on the image now, what we tend to see is not the view, but its edges—that tree-like texture applied to a two-dimensional surface. To the eyes of most contemporary players, this graveyard will not look particularly impressive. But what made the reviewer so excited was the *sense* of distance, the *feeling* of playful potentiality.

Two decades later, in 2017, Nintendo released the 19th entry in its Zelda series, *Breath of the Wild* (*BOTW*).[8] The kingdom of Hyrule expanded yet again, offering a painterly environment of forests, mountains, jungles, coastlines, and deserts. But the game starts, once again, with a cave. Link awakens in darkness. As he emerges into the misty daylight, the camera sweeps over him to reveal the world. The high horizon line foregrounds the landscape: a volcano towers ominously in the distance, and a castle stands in the center. The game's title appears in the corner, so as to not disturb the view.

The visuals, sound, pacing, and atmosphere all come together in this moment to offer what film scholar Aubrey Anable calls an "affective system."[9]

Introduction 3

Figure 1.2 Kakariko Village Graveyard in *The Legend of Zelda: Ocarina of Time.* Author screenshot.

Figure 1.3 Getting an overview in *The Legend of Zelda: Breath of the Wild.* Author screenshot.

It compels us to partake in a sublime moment; one that is difficult to articulate, but we intuit it at once. Encountering the sweeping landscape, we imagine an ideal of solitude and contemplation—clearly modeled after Caspar David Friedrich's *Wanderer Above the Sea of Fog*.

4 *Introduction*

Figure 1.4 Wanderer above the Sea of Fog, 1817, by Caspar David Friedrich. Kunsthalle Hamburg. Public domain, via Wikimedia Commons.

The history of *The Legend of Zelda* reveals a pattern of expansion and escalation. Where the 1986 game contains 128 overworld screens like the one depicted in Figure 1.1, and the map of *OOT* is about half a square kilometer in size, *BOTW* covers ca. 61 square kilometers, roughly the size of a small town.[10] Takumi Wada, the artist who created the official box art for the game, wrote that "I felt that the world itself, not just the character, had a leading role in this game."[11]

The turn to three-dimensional representation enabled new ways of imagining and advertising video games. Players were now able to explore virtual spaces with the same spatial dimensions as their daily lives, turning games from visual spectacles into meaningful virtual locations.[12] They could feel like they were part of the landscape as they traversed it; a sense of scope as they glanced at a map; a sense of power when getting an overview. Here, we find the origins of a slogan that summarizes the excitement of potential, freedom, and scope in games: *you can go there*. One early example can be found in the aforementioned review of *OOT*:

See that castle in the distance? You can run over to it, and a whole day will pass before you get there. See that river? You can follow it to its source, rooted in a whole new kingdom. See that huge mountain, ringed with clouds, miles and miles away? You can get right to the summit. And go inside. And fight a dragon.[13]

Variations of the phrase have been used in the promotional campaigns for a range of other games in the past decades, from *Tomb Raider*[14] to *No Man's Sky*,[15] *The Witcher 3*,[16] *Destiny*,[17] and *The Elder Scrolls: Skyrim*.[18] When the latter game was first shown at games conference E3 in 2011, director and producer Todd Howard pointed at a distant mountain, noting: "That mountain is not just a background—you can walk all the way to the top of that mountain."[19] Howard's quote would spur on countless memes and jokes repeated on forums and imageboards, revolving around the reassuring phrase "See that mountain? You can climb it."

This promise that *you can go there*, the central myth in this book, involves a tension between potential and constraints, between imagination and mediation. The hyperbolic nature of the slogan, however, leads to disappointment for players who take it too seriously. It can often be found on social media and message boards, associated with false advertising and empty promises. An early preview for *Destiny* had the developer overlooking a vista and noting, "This is coming straight out of our engine, all that stuff, if you ran out there, it's all playable terrain." When the final version of the game failed to fulfill this promise, fans speculated about why these features had been cut.[20] But it may be a more interesting question to ask why developers feel the need to make these claims to begin with. Why is the idea that *you can go there* such a convincing advertising strategy?

Why This Book

The *you can go there* myth reveals the extent to which advertisements and descriptions of video games borrow from the language of tourism.[21] They reference themes such as authenticity, strangerhood, colonialism, and the sublime—all of which are extensively covered in the field of tourism studies.

In the most basic sense, tourism entails the commodification of place: it provides the tourist with a sense of ownership over places simply by visiting and gazing at them. Tourism, in this context, is a system of symbolic performance: our attraction to a place arises from the socially constructed relationship between ourselves, the site, and its markers. As tourists, we desire to encounter what is "typical" of the place we visit. Successful tourist destinations offer essentialized, mythologized, or exoticized scenarios, which are often strategically scripted and deployed. When we go sightseeing, a collage of fantasies is opened up: in India you can find yourself, in Cuba you must dance the salsa, in African villages you encounter ancient cultures.

The fact that games are created as tourism sites means they are subject to similar types of structuring. As early as *Zork*,[22] in 1977, the player took on the guise of a treasure hunter "who is venturing into this dangerous land in search of wealth and adventure." This link between games and tourism is becoming more pertinent with every passing year. Having grown more graphically sophisticated, video games enable players to traverse landscapes, cities, islands, planets, and everything in between. Further, if we are to believe the messaging from technology companies such as Meta and Apple, games might also be a precursor to the future of virtual embodiment that awaits us. Connective technology aims to blend identities, social relations, and work across physical and virtual spaces of the metaverse. Given these corporate dreams of immersive virtuality, we would do well to ask how our current virtual environments are constructed, and what visiting them looks like when we actually do *go there*.

To answer these questions, I want to build on both tourism and game studies, discussing contemporary video games as forms of touristic advertising and experience. My approach is comparative, connecting and contrasting different games that deal with similar questions of touristic engagement. The reader will note, however, that these games differ substantially in terms of genre and mechanics. They include open-world action-adventure series such as Assassin's Creed, walking simulators such as *Firewatch*,[23] survival games such as *Minecraft*,[24] simulation games such as *Microsoft Flight Simulator 2020*,[25] and AR experiences such as *Pokémon Go*.[26] As game scholar Melissa Kagen notes, "game genre is not the only useful category for humanistic game scholarship, and sometimes it even blocks us from realizing the similarities among certain aspects of games in different ludic genres."[27]

Neither will I make a distinction between "adult" and "childish" games—whatever that distinction may mean. It is, however, worth noting that the story of Miyamoto's cave speaks to a sense of child-like wonder that ties to an enduring stigma around video games as a childish medium, even though the average player is 33[28] and plenty of games revolve around decidedly "adult" themes such as the nature of consciousness[29] or the decay of rural America under late capitalism.[30] I would say that the affective dimensions of games that are sometimes considered childish—like wonder, awe, and amazement—are often touristic fantasies in relatively undistilled forms.

If I seem to be conflating virtual and physical tourism, that is precisely my goal. Game studies scholars have long pointed out that the border between *viewing* and *experiencing* what happens on the screen is easily blurred. The hyphen in "player-character," as used to describe the avatar, highlights this corporeal synchronicity. Games researcher Katherine Isbister explains that as players move through the game world, they adopt their avatar's concerns and struggle toward the avatar's goals.[31] Players embed their avatars into their own bodily and perceptive schemas;[32] perhaps particularly so in three-dimensional games. I will talk about a "player-chacter" whenever this phenomenological overlap matters, and use the word "player" when referring to the person holding the controller or mouse. I will also use the second person pronoun "you" to highlight how games, not unlike tourism brochures, tend to offer a sense of imperative action.

I also want to connect this hybrid subjectivity to a particular type of *single-player experience*, which mirrors a specific type of touristic advertising. Both game spaces and touristic spaces can be constructed for solipsistic engagement, foregrounding the importance of individual experience. Think of the persistent use of the word "you" in tourism ads such as "You deserve Spain" or "Illinois – are you up for amazing?" Across the tourism industry, this logic of personalization and individual engagement is supported by algorithmic systems. These systems, through the increasing amount of data they are hoovering up, can produce granular and tailored *feeds*, built on recommendation systems, aggregated reviews, and real-time notifications for the digitally aided tourist.[33]

My focus in this book thus diverges from research in "virtual worlds" that primarily discusses these worlds as social spaces.[34] Game scholar Ralph Schroeder defines virtual worlds as "persistent virtual environments in which people experience others as being there with them—and where they can interact with them."[35] I focus on single-player environments as "worlds"—if only because many single-player games posit themselves as "worlds" for the player to explore. In fact, in keeping with the solipsistic sentiments of tourism, players are often supposed to be the only "subject in the world" in these games. Take the landscape in *BOTW* in Figure 1.3, which is completely devoid of other sightseers. This sense of subjective solitude, and the exclusive access that comes with it, is paralleled in the history of tourism.

Another difference between single and multiplayer games has to do with the degree of impact virtual visitors have on their environment. In her book on massively multiplayer online games (MMORPGs), Cecilia Pearce notes that players "play a part in actually shaping the world."[36] Yet the persistent presence of others also places limits on how mutable a game world can be. In MMORPGs, much like in theme parks, players might have shared experiences in their local groups or parties, but they typically cannot permanently impact the game world itself, as it always needs to be reset for the next group coming through. Single-player games, by contrast, are typically more malleable: entire landscapes, cities, or planets can be fundamentally altered by the efforts of the single player on some heroic quest. What influence do players have on the game world? How does this relate to the many sustainability issues that the tourism industry faces?

My claim is that video games can help us understand tourism, and that tourism can help us to understand video games. In the following chapters, I will focus on performative schemes—how you can move, what you can do, and whom you can meet—as types of touristic interaction.

I will analyze game mechanics, advertising discourses, reviews, and player responses (including my own), in order to explore how those spaces might encourage, inhibit, or resist us as tourists. Because they are virtual, game spaces can come to signify different things: resources to be exploited, escapist fantasies, sites for social interaction or community, a metaphor for psychological struggle, and so on.

I will argue that some of these signifiers allow for more responsible forms of tourism than others. Oftentimes, the myth that *you can go there* implies an attitude of certitude and entitlement couched in a long expansionist history. But games can also fight back against these assumptions. Sometimes, the world really is not that readily available. In the chapters to come, I want to show there is substantial potential in playing with and subverting touristic expectations in video games.

Chapter 2 covers the vocabulary of tourism and game studies that I will draw on. It explores the dependence of games on the "tourist gaze," and their use of player agency to enact these power structures. I also argue that the imaginative power of video games depends in large part on the increasing availability of the physical world; they offer "new frontiers" that hearken back to the colonial encounter. I introduce the key concept of defamiliarization, and discuss *Defective Holiday*[37] as a game that subverts the tourist gaze by excessively recruiting it.

Chapter 3 discusses different variations of the *you can go there* motif. It focuses on open-world games and explores the (missed) opportunities in this genre to defamiliarize players from common forms of gazing fostered by the scale of the game world. The Assassin's Creed series imagines player-characters as anti-tourists, hidden in the crowd; *The Legend of Zelda: Breath of the Wild* subverts its own focus on the sublime overview by insisting on detail-oriented attentiveness; *Elden Ring*[38] rejects the notion of an overview altogether.

Chapter 4 is oriented towards the walking simulator genre, which connects travel to the interiority of the mind. I focus on *The Stanley Parable*[39] as a game that exposes the myth of wayward independence that characterizes both tourism and gaming. I then explore walking sims that actually play with the physicality of movement: both *Journey*[40] and *Outer Wilds*[41] are examples of physics-oriented games that thereby grant players a sense of subversive control.

Chapter 5 discusses survival games such as *No Man's Sky* and *Minecraft*, which employ different means of spatial organization to create a sense of sublime peril. In the context of survival literature, these games foster a tourist gaze that is paradoxically oriented around labor. I also discuss a genre that seems opposed to the survival genre, in that is oriented towards building a home in an exotic location: life simulator games such as the Animal Crossing series.[42] I connect the popularity of these games and their use of gentle labor to the explosion of digital nomadism and other recent phenomena informed by a desire to lower the stakes of people's professional lives.

Chapter 6 focuses on games that elaborate on planet Earth by turning it into a site of leisurely, work-oriented, and imaginative travel. The games I cover in this chapter create specific types of (vehicular) embodiment through specific modalities of locomotion, which have already appeared in previous chapters: walking, driving, and flying. *Pokémon Go* offers a gamification of casual pedestrian movement; *Forza Horizon 5*[43] is an open-world racing game imagining Mexico as an emptied-out touristic dreamscape; *Microsoft Flight Simulator 2020* engages with the planet through the modern modality of flight. All of these games position the Earth as a backdrop for nomadic engagement while also keeping it at a distance.

Chapter 7 summarizes my argument. Focusing on games through a lens of tourism exposes them to productive criticism—specifically, around the ways in which they envision mobility and spatial constraints. The types of games we play, and the kinds of travel enacted in them, cannot be seen apart from how we think about our terrestrial trips, which are themselves gamified and algorithmically driven. Defamiliarization allows both designers and players to re-envision video games: not just as worlds to move around in but as experiences that have the potential to move us.

Notes

1 Nintendo EAD, *The Legend of Zelda*.
2 Stern Electronics, *Berzerk*.
3 E.g. Garriott, *Ultima 1*.
4 Parkin, "The Dazzling Reinvention of Zelda," para. 1.
5 Nintendo EAD, *The Legend of Zelda: Ocarina of Time*.
6 Overton, "The Legend of Zelda: Ocarina of Time," 46.
7 Overton, "The Legend of Zelda: Ocarina of Time," 48.
8 Nintendo EPD, *The Legend of Zelda: Breath of the Wild*.
9 Anable, *Playing with Feelings*, xii.
10 Webster, "Breath of the Wild's map."
11 Nintendo, *Creating a Champion*, 14.
12 Nitsche, "Video Game Spaces," 2.
13 Bickham, "The Legend of Zelda: Ocarina of Time," 43.
14 Crystal Dynamics, *Tomb Raider*.
15 Hello Games, *No Man's Sky*.
16 CD Projekt Red, *The Witcher*.
17 Bungie, *Destiny*.
18 Bethesda Game Studios, *The Elder Scrolls V: Skyrim*.
19 Bethesda Softworks, *The Elder Scrolls V: Skyrim—Demo Part 1*.
20 RefrigeratedFox, "The most disappointing thing about Destiny."
21 Dann, *The Language of Tourism*.
22 Infocom, *Zork*.
23 Campo Santo, *Firewatch*.
24 Mojang, *Minecraft*.
25 Asobo Studio, *Microsoft Flight Simulator*.
26 Niantic, *Pokémon Go*.
27 Kagen, *Wandering Games*, 176.
28 ESA, *Essential Facts*.
29 E.g. Croteam, *The Talos Principle*.
30 Cardboard Computer, *Kentucky Route Zero*.
31 Ibister, *How Games Move Us*, 11.
32 Crick, "The Game Body," 263–4.

33 Van Nuenen, *Scripted Journeys*.
34 Ensslin, "Looking Back"; Boellstorff et al., *Ethnography and Virtual Worlds*, 2.
35 Schroeder, "Defining Virtual Worlds and Virtual Environments."
36 Pearce, *Communities of Play*, 6.
37 Laughton, *Defective Holiday*.
38 FromSoftware, *Elden Ring*.
39 Galactic Café, *The Stanley Parable*.
40 Thatgamecompany, *Journey*.
41 Mobius Digital, *Outer Wilds*.
42 E.g. Nintendo EPD, *Animal Crossing: New Horizons*.
43 Playground Games, *Forza Horizon 5*.

References

Anable, Aubrey. *Playing with Feelings: Video Games and Affect*. Minneapolis: University of Minnesota Press, 2018.
Asobo Studio. *Microsoft Flight Simulator*. Xbox Game Studios. Microsoft Windows. 2020.
Bethesda Game Studios. *Fallout 3*. Bethesda Softworks. Microsoft Windows. 2008.
Bethesda Game Studios. *The Elder Scrolls IV: Oblivion*. Bethesda Softworks. Microsoft Windows. 2006.
Bethesda Game Studios. *The Elder Scrolls V: Skyrim*. Bethesda Softworks. Microsoft Windows. 2011.
Bethesda Softworks. "The Elder Scrolls V: Skyrim—Demo Part 1." YouTube, September 7, 2011, https://www.youtube.com/watch?v=5xwboyafbwc.
Bickham, Jes. "The Legend of Zelda: Ocarina of Time." *N64 Magazine* 24, January 1999, 32–45.
Boellstorff, Tom, Bonnie Nardi, Celia Pearce, and T.L. Taylor. *Ethnography and Virtual Worlds*. Princeton: Princeton University Press, 2012.
Bungie. *Destiny*. Activision. PlayStation 3. 2014.
Campo Santo. *Firewatch*. Campo Santo. PlayStation 4. 2016.
Cardboard Computer. *Kentucky Route Zero*. Annapurna Interactive. Microsoft Windows. 2020.
CD Projekt Red. *The Witcher 3: Wild Hunt*. CD Projekt. Xbox One. 2015.
Crick, Timothy. "The Game Body: Toward a Phenomenology of Contemporary Video Gaming." *Games and Culture* 6, no. 3 (2011): 259–69, doi:10.1177/1555412010364980.
Croteam. *The Talos Principle*. Devolver Digital. Microsoft Windows. 2014.
Crystal Dynamics. *Tomb Raider*. Square Enix. PlayStation 3. 2013.
Dann, Graham M.S. *The Language of Tourism: A Sociolinguistic Perspective*. Wallingford: CAB International, 1996.
Donlan, Christian. "'See Those Mountains?'" *Eurogamer.net*, June 16, 2014, https://www.eurogamer.net/articles/2014-06-12-see-those-mountains.
Ensslin, Astrid. "Looking Back: Ten Years of Editing Gaming and Virtual Worlds Scholarship." *Journal of Gaming & Virtual Worlds* 10, no. 1 (2018): 3–5, doi:10.1386/jgvw.10.1.3_2.
ESA. *Essential Facts about the Video Game Industry 2022*. Entertainment Software Association, https://www.theesa.com/resource/2022-essential-facts-about-the-video-game-industry/.

FromSoftware. *Elden Ring*. Bandai Namco Entertainment. Microsoft Windows. 2022.
Galactic Café. *The Stanley Parable*. Galactic Café. Microsoft Windows. 2013.
Garriott, Richard. *Ultima 1*. California Pacific. Apple II. 1981.
Giant Sparrow. *What Remains of Edith Finch*. Annapurna Interactive. Microsoft Windows. 2016.
Hello Games. *No Man's Sky*. Hello Games. PlayStation 4. 2016.
Ibister, Katherine. *How Games Move Us: How Games Move Us Emotion by Design*. Cambridge: MIT Press, 2013.
Infocom. *Zork*. Personal Software, Infocom, Activision. PDP-10. 1980.
Kagen, Melissa. *Wandering Games*. Cambridge: MIT Press, 2022.
Laughton, Kim. *Defective Holiday*. Kim Laughton. Microsoft Windows. 2020.
Mobius Digital. *Outer Wilds*. Annapurna Interactive. Microsoft Windows. 2019.
Mojang. *Minecraft*. Mojang. Microsoft Windows. 2011.
Niantic. *Pokémon Go*. Niantic. iOS. 2016.
Nintendo. *The Legend of Zelda: Breath of the Wild-Creating a Champion Hero's Edition*. Milwaukie: Dark Horse Comics, 2018.
Nintendo EAD. *The Legend of Zelda: Ocarina of Time*. Nintendo. Nintendo 64. 1998.
Nintendo EAD. *The Legend of Zelda*. Nintendo. NES. 1986.
Nintendo EPD. *The Legend of Zelda: Breath of the Wild*. Nintendo. Nintendo Switch. 2017.
Nintendo EPD. *Animal Crossing: New Horizons*. Nintendo. Nintendo Switch. 2020.
Nitsche, Michael. *Video Game Spaces: Image, Play, and Structure in 3D Worlds*. Cambridge: MIT Press, 2008.
Overton, Wil. "The Legend of Zelda: Ocarina of Time." *N64 Magazine* 23 (UK), December 1998, 42–49.
Parkin, Simon. "The Dazzling Reinvention of Zelda." *The New Yorker*, March 8, 2017, https://www.newyorker.com/tech/annals-of-technology/the-dazzling-reinvention-of-zelda.
Pearce, Celia, and Artemesia. *Communities of Play: Emergent Cultural in Multiplayer Games and Virtual Worlds*. Cambridge: MIT Press, 2009.
Playground Games. *Forza Horizon 5*. Xbox Game Studios. Microsoft Windows. 2021.
RefrigeratedFox. "The Most Disappointing Thing about Destiny." YouTube, September 12, 2014, https://www.youtube.com/watch?v=V9YoJjdEBv8.
Rockstar North. *Grand Theft Auto V*. Rockstar Games. PlayStation 3. 2013.
Schroeder, Ralph. "Defining Virtual Worlds and Virtual Environments." *Journal For Virtual Worlds Research* 1, no. 1 (2008), doi:10.4101/jvwr.v1i1.294.
SCS Software. *Euro Truck Simulator 2*. SCS Software. Microsoft Windows. 2012.
Sheff, David. *Game Over: How Nintendo Conquered The World*. New York: Random House, 1993.
Stern Electronics. *Berzerk*. Stern Electronics. Atari 2600. 1980.
thatgamecompany. *Journey*. Sony Computer Entertainment. PlayStation 3. 2012.
Ubisoft Montreal. *Assassin's Creed Valhalla*. Ubisoft. Microsoft Windows. 2020.
Ubisoft North America. "Assassin's Creed Valhalla: Discovery Tour – Viking Age." YouTube, October 19, 2021, https://www.youtube.com/watch?v=2A8vES0EwOY.
Ubisoft Toronto. *Far Cry 6*. Ubisoft. Microsoft Windows. 2021.
Van Nuenen, Tom. *Scripted Journeys*. Berlin: De Gruyter, 2021.

Webster, Andrew. "The Legend of Zelda: Breath of the Wild's Map Is Based on Kyoto." *The Verge*, March 6, 2017, https://www.theverge.com/2017/3/6/14827832/the-legend-of-zelda-breath-of-the-wild-map-kyoto-japan.

Youngs, Tim. "Travel Writing After 1900." In *The Cambridge History of Travel Writing*, edited by Nandini Das and Tim Youngs, 125–39. Cambridge: Cambridge University Press, 2019.

Zynga. *Farmville*. Zynga. HTML5. 2009.

2 It's All Under Control

The *you can go there* slogan underlines that playing games is a touristic endeavor, and that tourism is becoming an obvious commercial framework for advertising video games. This chapter is largely theoretical, covering the critical vocabulary of tourism studies that I will draw on when analyzing different permutations of the slogan. Thinking about games as forms of tourism means asking questions about expansionism, consumption, and immersion—questions that are covered in game studies as well.

I view tourism through a constructionist lens—that is, I stress the social or intersubjective process in the construction of knowledge and reality. Touristic activity, in this context, consists of symbolic markers—signs or symbols carrying specific meaning within a particular socio-cultural context—erected around tourist cities or countries. What this often comes down to is the creation of stereotyped images and expectations held by the members of the societies that can afford to send out tourists.[1] Activities become signifiers of "typical cultural practice": the rude behavior of a Frenchman becomes a sign of Frenchness, an English pub becomes a sign of the country's drinking culture. This is the kind of work you are supposed to do as a tourist. "All over the world," wrote Jonathan Culler, "[tourists] are engaged in reading cities, landscapes and cultures as sign systems."[2] Crucially, these myths retain their power because we are only at our destinations temporarily—long enough to be reminded of them, and short enough for them not to be punctured.

The word *myth*, in this context, refers to communicative forms that a society uses to convey and reinforce its values and beliefs, often unconsciously. The literary theorist Roland Barthes highlighted how myths naturalize the cultural, social, and political norms of a society. They make certain aspects of the world seem universally true, while in fact they are culturally constructed.[3] Myths are readily found in branding and advertising: they build on and reinforce existing norms around what is supposed to be a desirable experience.

Take an advertisement of a pristine beach with crystal clear waters, lined with palm trees and a hammock strung between them: it suggests an idyllic paradise where one can escape from the pressures and realities of everyday life. It brings into view a whole range of values and desires associated with leisure, escape, and luxury, and it ignores the question of whether this beach may in fact be commercialized, crowded, or causing environmental issues. Tourism is built on such kinds of promotional texts, which attempt to "persuade, lure, woo and seduce millions of human beings, and, in doing so, convert them from potential into actual clients."[4]

How does this come into play for the individual tourist? Sociologist John Urry elaborated on this interplay of imagination and reality through what he called the *tourist gaze*: the set of expectations, perceptions, and behaviors that tourists adopt when engaging with and interpreting new environments and cultures during their travels. The tourist gaze is not just visual, but formed by a range of performative, embodied practices that "organize the encounters of visitors with the 'other,' providing some sense of competence, pleasure and structure to those experiences."[5]

Urry's concept is inspired by the French philosopher Michel Foucault, who wrote that gazing implies a form of power. Foucault was interested in the medical gaze: this is not just a physical act of looking, but includes the way in which society constructs knowledge and meaning through systems of observation, categorization, and surveillance. The tourist gaze is a similar system of dominance, related to histories of colonial exploration and conquest, as well as current socio-economic disparities between tourists and the places they visit. It leads certain locations, cultures, and experiences to be highlighted and commodified for tourists, while others are left unseen. Marketers eagerly rely on the stories, images, and desires of the world's destinations and activities, without which, as Salazar and Graburn note, "there probably would be little tourism."[6]

Video games have taken cues from the tourist gaze since the dawn of early text adventure games. In 1980, *Zork*[7] occasionally took the form of a tourist brochure. Emerging from a forest, the game describes a splendid vista with a hint of irony:

> You are at the top of the Great Canyon on its west wall. From here there is a marvelous view of the canyon and parts of the Frigid River upstream. Across the canyon, the walls of the White Cliffs join the mighty ramparts of the Flathead Mountains to the east. Following the Canyon upstream to the north, Aragain Falls may be seen, complete with rainbow. The mighty Frigid River flows out from a great dark cavern. To the west and south can be seen an immense forest, stretching for miles around.

A lot has changed since 1980. The spatial structures that programmers are able to create have expanded from elemental "contained" spaces to the two-dimensional "scrolling" planes of the 1980s and 1990s and finally to the third dimension.[8] Textual narrativization is no longer needed. In 2019, Microsoft launched a tourism campaign, called *Visit Xbox*, to highlight the graphical capacity of its Xbox One X console (see Figure 2.1). The campaign involved a 70-second film in the style of a tourist board advertisement, with sun-soaked beaches, mountain ranges, and cityscapes over a meditative soundtrack. In

It's All Under Control 15

2020, *Rough Guides* released a guidebook of gaming worlds, such as the lost city of Paititi in *Shadow of the Tomb Raider*, and the region of Arkadia in *Assassin's Creed: Odyssey*. In a blog post, the *Rough Guides* editors wrote:

> For a long time, video games [...] just weren't that immersive. [...] That distinction has now been eroded. Game graphics are so immersive and all-consuming, you don't just experience the gameplay—you experience the very world in which the gameplay unfolds. That thrilling feeling of being somewhere new is no longer the exclusive domain of real-world travel.[9]

Campaigns such as *Visit Xbox*[10] might be the ideal example of what André Bazin once called the myth of Total Cinema. In Bazin's vision, the history of film could be seen as a progressive movement toward an ultimate goal: "a total and complete representation of reality ... the reconstruction of a perfect illusion of the outside world in sound, color, and relief ... a recreation of the world in its own image, an image unburdened by the freedom of interpretation of the artist or the irreversibility of time."[11]

Bazin's ultimate goal speaks to the paradox of the map and the territory—the relationship between an object and a representation of that object, as in

Figure 2.1 *Visit Xbox* advertisement. Author screenshot.

the relation between a geographical territory and a map of it. The problem is captured in Lewis Carroll's *Sylvie and Bruno*,[12] in which one of the characters takes map-making to its logical extreme:

> "That's another thing we've learned from your Nation," said Mein Herr, "map-making. But we've carried it much further than you. What do *you* consider the *largest* map that would be really useful?"
> "About six inches to the mile."
> "Only *six inches!*" exclaimed Mein Herr. "We very soon got to six yards to the mile. Then we tried a *hundred* yards to the mile. And then came the grandest idea of all! We actually made a map of the country, on the scale of a *mile to the mile!*"
> "Have you used it much?" I enquired.
> "It has never been spread out, yet," said Mein Herr: "the farmers objected: they said it would cover the whole country, and shut out the sunlight! So we now use the country itself, as its own map, and I assure you it does nearly as well."

Endearing as the naiveté of Mein Herr might be, his belief is the logical endpoint of the *you can go there* myth. It promises a total representation, a sense of "immersion" in which, as the *Visit Xbox* ad notes, you "experience the very world in which the gameplay unfolds." It is this concept of immersion that I want to discuss in this chapter.

Pixels and Passports

The Western idea of travel has long been associated with the adventure of entering unfamiliar or unknown territory. The myth of exploration involves navigating uncharted seas or traversing vast spaces, often without being able to know or even imagine the destination. For players and tourists alike, "having the world at your feet" is a power fantasy hearkening back to the growth of capitalism and the rise of European colonial expansion.

Mary Fuller and Henry Jenkins wrote that there are striking parallels between the rhetoric of virtual exploration and that of Renaissance travel writing on the New World. The territories beyond the player's current grasp, like the megabytes in the game's executable file, "exist only in the abstract, as potential sites for narrative action, as locations that have not yet been colonized [...] Places become meaningful only as they come into contact with narrative agents."[13] Indeed, developers, players, the popular media, and academic researchers have often resorted to historically loaded metaphors of "new worlds" or "new frontiers" when describing video games, implicating the European colonial encounter with the Americas.[14] In other words, the potentiality of *you can go there* often builds on the colonial imagination.

At the same time, the reality of travel looks somewhat different: it takes place in a world that is comprehensively known and mapped. Over a few decades, the expanding middle classes of the Global North have achieved greatly increased access to air and sea travel around the world. Globalization and mobility, for them, have gone hand in hand. While digital technology has made travel more accessible, it has also shifted our expectations of what it means to be a tourist. We no longer simply traverse physical spaces but also navigate an intricate network of global communication systems, from booking websites to review platforms and translation apps.

These tools, while making travel more efficient and affordable, also shape our perceptions and experiences of the places we visit. Our experiences are not only mediated by technology, but shaped by the algorithms that guide our movements, extend our cognitive capacities, and reduce language barriers. However, this new landscape of digital tourism comes with its own set of challenges. As our decision-making becomes increasingly dependent on personalized recommendations through predictive modeling and pervasive viral trends, the Romantic dream of encountering the unfamiliar or the unknown is becoming more difficult to realize.

Our world's increasing predictability has created a new set of touristic objectives. This is perhaps most evident in the countless systems of gamification one finds in platforms such as TripAdvisor, booking.com, and Airbnb. The ubiquitous collection of points and levels in these systems is intended to give users a sense of control over the experience: they are *leveling up* while checking in, taking photos, or leaving reviews. These platforms not only allow us access to "insider" knowledge about places we have never been, but they also enable us to start weighing in as "insiders" from the moment we land. Travel is not just about exploration, but about *optimization*, and about documenting our successes towards that end.

Yet, beneath this seemingly empowering user experience lies a surreptitious form of informatic control. While the promise of fine-tuned customization offered by these apps is seductive, they ultimately foster their own forms of digital dependence: consumers are often found glued to these apps while traveling. Platforms become mediators of our experiences, directing our actions and perceptions in line with their built-in algorithms and reward systems. The act of earning points, leveling up, or attaining virtual badges subtly shapes our behaviors, making us conform to the dictates of the platform. The control of these apps is not overt or directly oppressive, but pervasively embedded in our routines and habits.

Both in the context of gamified systems and video games proper, the formative concept here is that of immersion. Digital media scholar Janet Murray describes it as "the sensation of being surrounded by a completely other reality, as different as water is from air, that takes over all of our attention, our whole perceptual apparatus."[15] While there is no academic consensus around a definition of immersion, or how to quantify its effects, popular culture almost universally equates "more immersion" with "better experiences." In fact, the history of gamification and immersion is a history of creating purportedly superior consumer experiences to those supplied by the physical world. Edward Castronova once predicted that the rise of then-popular shared virtual worlds such as *Second Life*[16] would one day lead to a "virtual exodus." He argued that people seek out fun, and virtual worlds are designed to be fun: hence, within a few decades, our society would take all the best cues from video games and leave people with little reason to stay in the physical world.[17]

The claims about shared virtual world environments largely died down as the user base of *Second Life* dwindled. Yet they were recently resuscitated with the corporate interest in the "metaverse" as the next stage in the development of the internet—for instance, by Facebook's showy corporate rebranding into Meta in 2021, or Apple's introduction of its AR headset as a form of "spatial computing."[18] Mark Zuckerberg suggested we view the metaverse as an embodied internet "where instead of just viewing content—you are in it."[19] While the future of the metaverse seems unclear, it points to the increased blending of identities, work, and sociality across physical and virtual spaces.

It has been often noted that the success of the metaverse mainly will depend on its immersive quality. As a 2021 *Vanity Fair* article put it, immersion needs to reach the point at which "it becomes ambiguous if you're in reality or hanging out in the metaverse."[20] These perennial promises about the impending inability to distinguish virtuality from the "real world" are couched in a long-standing—and false—dichotomy between online and offline, and more basically, nature and technology. What they assume is that "full immersion" means losing the ability to discern the virtual from the real. But virtual worlds, like social media, will not be more engaging because we do not even realize we are inhabiting them. If we choose to immerse ourselves in them, it will be because they offer us a package of intensified symbolic interaction. This is not just about having more *fun*, as Castronova argued. It is about more anxiety, more antagonism, and more one-upmanship as well. Beyond asking how to maximize immersion, we should wonder to what ends we are being immersed.

Essentially, messaging around the metaverse hints at a more thoroughly connected commercialized lifestyle. It seems wise to ask critical questions about how data rights, privacy, and security will be safeguarded. More to the point of this book, these interoperable virtual environments are not just abstract spaces, but places for *dwelling*—that is, creating meaning, asserting agency, and carving out your own personal spaces.[21] We need to think about what kind of dwelling we want. This question immediately takes us to the realm of gaming, where metaverse properties have been in effect for years.

Take *Fortnite*, the immensely popular survival game with over 350 million registered players. In February 2021, the game hosted a film festival screened on in-game cinema screens, and in September of the same year it hosted a three-week-long concert series, attended concurrently by some 12 million players. *Fortnite* is not simply a game; it resembles platforms like Facebook in that it has evolved into an infrastructure,[22] incrementally reconfiguring itself based on user metrics and feedback. It is built on strategically forged partnerships (such as 2018's Marvel crossover), and embeds itself in other markets, domains, and fandoms.

Fortnite is just one instance of how video games can transform into platforms for wider engagement and dwelling. Another example is *Roblox*, a platform where users can create and sell their own games: near the end of 2021, it was valued at about $30 billion at the New York Stock Exchange and drawing in about 40 million daily users, most of them children between 9 and 12 years old. The popularity of *Roblox* can be directly connected to the coronavirus pandemic and the difficulty of physical travel, and there are plenty of reasons to believe these platforms will only continue to grow in scope. Whenever we talk about the popularity of these platforms, we should keep in mind that it is not just because of pull factors, but push factors as well. That is, the inhospitality of the physical world also has an influence on the appeal of virtual platforms. Climate science makes it plainly evident that we stand a high chance of inheriting a world of ecological struggle—if not disaster—in which virtuality may be the safest and most tenable approach to social contact and travel. In the worst-case scenario, *we can go there* only because there is nowhere else to go.

Further, there are obvious financial interests at play when platform infrastructures like *Roblox* implement systems of standardized interoperability. Web3 and cryptocurrency enthusiasts speculate that the future of gaming will involve the authenticated ownership of in-game goods as non-fungible tokens, effortlessly moving across platforms and services. Much like the current-day loot boxes or *gacha* mechanics, which implement mechanics akin to toy vending machines, these systems will no doubt be put in place to keep players invested in the ecologies they are spending time in. Existing revenue models such as "play-to-earn" already reward players with content or cryptocurrencies for playing: for instance, privacy-sensitive browser Brave offers users cryptocurrency as a reward for watching ads, and *Roblox* content creators can convert their digital "robux," earned by the sales of their games, to cash. We can expect further convergence of digital and non-digital currencies, risking further social stratification and the commodification of social life.

The metaverse is, according to Mark Zuckerberg, still at least a decade away, and it may well turn out to be a passing fad. Gamification and immersive environments, however, are here to stay—and here to be iterated upon, to be made more efficient and addictive. It is crucial to think about ways in which games are keeping us immersed, and what kinds of values we want to encode in the virtual environments of the future.

The Issue with Flow

Both in the scholarship and media discourse on games, discussions of immersion are unavoidably accompanied by Mihaly Csikszentmihalyi's psychological concept of flow, the experience of intense absorption. The concept emerged from Csikszentmihalyi's research into the foundations of play, creativity, and enjoyment as reported by mountain climbers, musicians, surgeons, athletes, and others. All of them described the experience of being swept up and carried away by an activity they thoroughly enjoyed. Csikszentmihalyi summarized this state as an "optimal experience" that characterizes "the best moments in our lives." We encounter it when we engage in autotelic—that is, internally driven—activities in which our skills are balanced with challenges, experienced as the harmonious ordering of consciousness.[23]

Yet, as media scholar Braxton Soderman pointed out, flow needs to be understood as an ideological concept as much as an optimal psychological state. Csikszentmihalyi, who witnessed the Soviet attack and occupation of Hungary at the end of World War II, conceived of it as an alternative to the lure of Marxism. He argued that individuals within Western democracies could only be motivated to overcome alienation through the empowerment of individual consciousness.[24] Soderman writes that this idea brings a very particular kind of media consumer into being—one that "privileges individuality over social collectivities, growth and accumulation over equilibrium and sustainability, self-determination over the idea that external forces shape human consciousness and action over critical examination."[25]

"Harmonious consciousness," in other words, is tied to the most questionable corners of our consumptive lives. Social media platforms keep users in a state of flow by eliciting negative emotions[26] and most impulse purchases are made in a flow state.[27] In sum, flow is often used to intensify playful consumption, extend playtimes, and foster addiction. Flow connects play to tourism in many ways. Both take place in a temporary environment, are marked by additional challenges—which can be as small as finding a restaurant or trying new food—and incite feelings of immersion and intensity.[28]

Tellingly, Csikszentmihalyi has also written about flow in tourism. Beyond the skill-based forms of recreation that tourists engage in, he and his co-author John K. Coffey mention smaller "microflow" activities such as practicing one's Spanish in a restaurant, making French toast in the morning without the distractions of everyday life, or being in tune during a "great intimacy session."[29]

The title of the authors' article, "Finding Flow," suggests that flow is just there, waiting to be discovered. It neglects the ways in which this flow is part of the predesigned consumer experience. The ideal tourist, after all, is constantly in a state of flow—from buying perfume at a duty-free shop, to breaking into the hotel minibar, to being absorbed in a guided tour. Even the more "self-dependent" modes of travel are characterized by apps and services such as TripAdvisor that promise a frictionless experience that one can attend to *on the spot*—for instance, to find a city's hidden gems.[30] In sum, as Helen Kennedy suggests, "flow is not so much about a state of perfect control but more a perfect submission to [ζ] technologies."[31] In games and in tourism

It's All Under Control 21

alike, the control of the player/tourist is always encapsulated within a controlled system. It is this dual sense of control that I want to explore further: it offers productive ways to think about the tourist structures in which we are so commonly entangled.

An Unsettling Vacation

Defective Holiday[32] starts with a spherical orb against a serene white backdrop. It looks a bit like a crystal ball, except it has an orange sticker with the game's title on it. Looking inside it, there are images of touristic capstones: tropical islands, some tents pitched on a mountain range. But curiously, the fortunes it tells are not all spectacular: there are also airport customs stanchions and in-flight entertainment screens. You hear the voice of a salesperson claiming they really shouldn't be selling this experience, that it was previously returned by some customer who had complained that "it wasn't working correctly." But, as in most tourist purchases, an exception will be made for you, and so you are transported inside.

The first scene starts on a scenic mountain path. As you walk up the hill, you hear glossy electronic elevator music as your footsteps are hitting the soil. The landscape is beautiful, but also strangely fraudulent: it distorts and wavers outside of your radius, and seems to be assembled right in front of you. It is clear that all of this is a construct.

Pedestrian direction signage urges you along the preset path. As you approach its end, a low, uncomfortable noise begins to hum beneath the agreeable synthesizers. You reach a grave with flowers, and a shovel sticking in the

Figure 2.2 Following the route in *Defective Holiday*. Author screenshot.

sand. The screen whites out, and the low noise intensifies. You hear digging sounds. When your sight returns, you appear to have dug up a red coffin. Your only option is to click on it; it opens to reveal a pile of passenger arrival cards. The scene ends.

Defective Holiday offers a series of these kinds of unsettling tourist vignettes. Developed by 3D artist and graphic designer Kim Laughton, it depicts the episodic and alienating nature of the tourist experience. In the second scene, you are standing on a misty airport runway with the sound of airplanes buzzing by. There is a towable passenger stairway in front of you, but the associated plane seems to have departed. As you explore the disorienting scene, it becomes clear there is nothing in particular the game expects you to do; the confusing taxiway markings on the ground guide you around in circles.

Like touristic experiences, the fragments in *Defective Holiday* succeed each other at a set pace. The game takes about 45 minutes to complete and becomes increasingly disorienting and ominous in the process. Interactive scenes are interspersed with images from travel advertisements, such as real-life footage of coconut trees, or a sunglass-wearing tourist heroically posing next to a bright blue four-wheel drive. Through its scenarios, the game wavers between mundanity and absurdity. You sit in a taxi. You stand at a baggage claim area next to a sign saying "BAGS LOOK ALIKE." You look through a camera screen with an excessive number of icons, pointed at a tourist in swimming shorts behind a cardboard cutout of a carrot. All the while there is unassertive advertorial music playing, highlighting your ambivalent, ironic connection to this world. The non-player characters' voices seem knowingly overacted when offering their rehearsed platitudes. The taxi driver noting that "it's nice to buy the same things in a new place," the tourist lounging on a tropical beach complaining that "there's not much to do on this island"—they all sound like bored thespians in a fever dream.

Laughton's work is dream-like, associative, Lynchian. Its structure of reality seems constantly at risk. One reviewer of the game noted: "I could never shake the feeling that I was in peril even though I was never in danger."[33] The scenes are littered with recurring symbols of both mundanity and violence. A machete appearing from an airport scanner; a washed-up pedalo at a mountain trail; a lifeless tourist in an airport hall with the machete in his back. As the game progresses, some of these elements start to recur. You come across a previously tidy tourist site, now derelict. You find the previously deceased tourist alive and well on an airport bench with a meek smile. Next to him is a cart of cleaning products and a cordoned-off section of the floor where you found his body, now scrubbed clean. Disaster is barely hidden from view, and the sense of dread is only amplified by Laughton's glossy, polished graphics. The 3D modeling is both uncannily realistic and consistently foregrounding its artifice.

It is as though the game wants you to employ the tourist gaze, priming you for aesthetic experience only in order to disrupt it. It seems to consume the tourist gaze itself, acting as a disorienting response to the common appetite for beautiful sights. It is through this carnival of middle-class obsessions and absurd violence that we get to see the contrivance of tourism, and how incredibly boring it can be. One of the game's reviewers on digital distribution service Steam wrote disappointedly that "This is essentially a 3D Modeler's portfolio piece [but] there is zero interactivity, beyond moving and looking around with the mouse." They are right: *Defective Holiday* plays with the recognizability of tourist encounters, and explicitly forces players onto a preset, yet ultimately disorienting path. It tells us that there is a silent preposterousness to the whole endeavor if we care to look closer.

Defective Holiday introduces confusion into leisure habits that most of us perform on autopilot. It is a great example of the type of thinking that offers an alternative to the frictionless consumption of space that both video games and tourism commonly provide us with. We need more of this kind of thinking in gaming—not only to make better games, but to modify our gaze. If there is one thing the tourist can learn from the player, it is a form of being unsettled, or as the Russian Formalists called it, *defamiliarized*.[34]

Defamiliarizing Play

Jacques Derrida wrote of play as a looseness, in the sense that a string not pulled taut has play.[35] His comments come close to the definitions of play currently used in game studies: game designers Katie Salen and Eric Zimmerman, for instance, define play as "free movement within a more rigid structure."[36] It is this free movement that is emphasized in the promise that *you can go there*. Indeed, video game players often come to a game space with a strong sense of agency. This is because, in contrast to our physical lives, player-characters inhabit worlds specifically made for their abilities. As games scholar James Paul Gee notes, when we play a stealth game in which an avatar is good at hiding, the game world generally offers plenty of scenery to hide behind. "The world is good at being hidden in."[37]

Games, in other words, provide the framework in which we make sense of what happens; they create both the context and content for meaning. Interacting with game objects, players develop hypotheses about what degree of freedom they have, and which potential strategies they could employ. James Gibson's psychological concept of *affordances* is often used in this context. Affordances are the possibilities for action that the environment provides to an individual.[38] A chair affords sitting, a cup affords holding liquid, a button affords pushing, and so on. In creating a range of specific affordances for the player, games are able to communicate rhetorically—and, by extension, ideologically.

Playing a game, one expects that the abilities one is given will have a purpose within the environment. The expectation that skills and spaces will be congruent stimulates a particularly intense form of the tourist gaze. If the tourist is defined by their search for signs of what is "typical" of a place, the player goes one step further, joining into the systematized, prescribed logic of interaction. Signifiers become something directly *actionable*. If you see a cave, you expect that the game wants you to enter it. If you see a tower, you expect that the game wants you to climb it.

So, while players come to a game with a strong sense of agency, the activity of playing a game consists of particular forms of submission. For a long time, scholars of games and play have pointed out how, when players step into the magic circle of play, they agree to abide by the unique rules and space-time of the game, and temporarily set aside their everyday concerns.[39] Philosopher Hans-Georg Gadamer wrote that we think of ourselves as subjects playing the game, but that while we are doing so, submit ourselves to a game's logic and ruleset. It would be more accurate to say that we are the ones being played.[40]

That is not to say, however, that players cannot subvert what a game "expects" them to do. Shira Chess writes in *Play Like a Feminist* that playing can be a tool for radical disruption, allowing us to envision new strategies to overcome political and cultural oppression.[41] Think of the massively popular practice of speedrunning—completing a game as quickly as possible—which is often accompanied by a discourse of *destroying* or *breaking* a game. Indeed, speedrunning inverts a power dynamic: game developers now frequently create reaction videos on YouTube gasping at the machinic efficacy with which expert players complete their creation.[42] The allure of *metagaming* and speedrunning, as Shira Chess emphasizes, is about agency. It connects the specifics of gameplay to "the will to act and gain voice in a system of power."[43] But while these kinds of practices might "break the game," they do not break the magic circle. The game is still there; breaking the rules is only fun because the rules exist.

The thrill of subversive play is relevant to tourism as well. Tourism paradoxically urges its subjects to go "off the beaten track," follow their own whims, and encounter the authentic Other. Further, both games and tourism benefit from a sense of conspicuous consumerism and atomism, in which individuals can imagine themselves as being somehow different from everyone around them. This is evident when witnessing tourists get out of each other's way when taking pictures of a landmark, so it looks like they were alone. As Walker Percy summarized, "the more lookers, the less there is to see."[44] Even the more mundane forms of contemporary tourism include a sense of autonomy and self-efficacy through the promise of tailored, personalized, customized experiences. Contemporary, digitally aided tourism is a network of autonomous social actors within broader systems of informatic control.

Philosopher Alexander Galloway has discussed this paradox of controlled mobilities. He builds on Gilles Deleuzes' distinction between high modernity—characterized by central bureaucracies and vertical hierarchies—and the contemporary, networked "societies of control" in which subtle, diffuse mechanisms allow for controlled mobility by autonomous social actors. Galloway sees video games as the emblematic example of this shift: they work by virtue of having players internalize and become intimate with its algorithmic rules. Galloway writes how games flaunt their informatic control instead of hiding it: "To play the game means to play the code of the game. To win means to know the system."[45] It is this ideological completion that games require of their players that interests me—particularly in the context of travel. What kind of tourist gaze are players expected to come to a game with? What kind of spatial appropriation are they expected to engage in?

I would argue that taking this perspective can help designers and marketeers to think more critically about their work. My goal here is also to offer an alternative to the prevailing approach of categorizing player types and motivations. To give an example, one of the most frequently cited works in game design is Richard Bartle's 1996 paper on player types.[46] This taxonomy includes *achievers* (who want to pass the challenge of a game and achieve its goals), *socializers* (who are interested in relationships with other people), *killers* (who want to impose themselves on others), and, pertinently, *explorers*. This last type, according to Bartle, wants most of all to get to know the breadth of the game and discover its inner machinations. Bartle gives an example of players wanting to min-max a game by finding the shortest route from point A to B.

Player typologies like these are no doubt popular because game designers and marketers can make use of them: psychographic and behavioral segmentation is a fundamental part of game design.[47] The goal of segmentation is to better serve customers by being able to offer products that match their needs and wants. Bartle has been criticized that his typology is too simplistic, and that people's behavior and motivations can change over time and across different contexts. The main issue that I want to point to, though, is that there is something circular about typecasting players in this way. Player typologies are often defined by the same kind of utilitarian logic that drives games. Bartle's definition of "explorers," for instance, is typically masculine-coded; it also derives from the earlier mentioned systems of colonialism and control that have been thoroughly encoded in the medium. Exploration here is a utilitarian form of exerting control over the game and min-maxing that, in turn, reinforces the touristic *modus operandi* I have been critiquing. If game designers write games geared towards Bartle's explorer, they will create worlds that afford conquering.

I want to take a different approach, and ask what happens when the game creates affordances for players to step outside of these familiar ways of playing. In much the same way that *Defective Holiday* confuses players by complicating the leisure habits that we usually perform on autopilot, games have the potential to disrupt the ideological goals that inform the way we approach game worlds, and by extension, the physical world.

Offering a much-needed alternative view on exploration, Melissa Kagen has recently examined what she calls wandering games: "games that are interested in alternative modes of expression, embodiment, environment, orientation, and community."[48] She situates the genre of walking simulators (which I discuss in Chapter 4) in the intellectual history of walking. Wandering, she notes, can be a political act of resistance; it can foment radically unproductive, contemplative, and anticapitalist forms of play. Of course, one might argue that this "wanderer" is simply another player type to be inserted in a typology. But the point is not to essentialize the alternative modes of expression Kagen discusses. It is to unsettle the normatively charged goals that players come to a game with.

As I have been arguing, games can algorithmically model the tourist gaze. This involves the familiarization of the strange—for instance, by describing non-Western peoples and places in terms of Western histories.[49] The slogan *you can go there* promises something that begins as something potentially exploitative. The "you" is the subject who is lured into forms of playing that do not allow for unthinking, subversion, and self-reflection.

However, I am also interested in exploring games that recruit the tourist gaze in order to subvert it.

In discussing these games, I draw on the Russian Formalist concept of defamiliarization. The literary critic Viktor Shklovsky held that the purpose of art is to make the familiar seem strange, to make us see common things as if for the first time. He believed that habitualization dulled our perception of the world, causing us to overlook what he called the "sensation of life." Defamiliarization serves as a tool for artists and writers to jolt readers out of their habitual experience and thus to perceive the world anew.

The principle of defamiliarization runs against the economizing of attention and comprehension by art: it highlights how art transgresses the limits of habitual perception, facilitating a novel understanding of some aspect of the world. As a formalistic endeavor, it requires devices by which objects can be robbed of their usual associations, in order to keep the strange intact as something strange.[50] Shklovsky writes that "the process of perception is an aesthetic end in itself and must be prolonged."

To Shklovsky, this prolonging of perception has to do with both *difficulty* and *length*. Both of these terms are relevant in the context of video game reception. First of all, Shklovsky allows us to reconsider our common understanding of "difficult games" as a matter of manual dexterity and aptitude. At the same time, difficulty is not necessarily about intellectualist trappings, either. Shklovsky calls for perceptions that do not immediately make sense through established categories of thought, like the absurd juxtaposition of gondolas and coffins in *Defective Holiday*.

The concept of length, similarly, is not a function of the game world but of our perception. Games have long been judged based on "how long" they are; whether a game is worth the cost of purchase is often deemed to be dependent on how many hours the player can expect to spend inside of it. What Shklovsky brings to mind, however, is the length of our attention span—the extent to which we pay attention to something before being distracted by something else.

Defamiliarization, both as a design practice and as a way of engaging with games, means subverting the normative, common-sensical ways in which they are expected to play out. In the context of tourism, it means complicating and reorienting the tourist gaze, upon which many games are founded. I think we need to be optimistic: games can do more than imagine us as settlers in a brave new world. That is, they can *unsettle* us.

Notes

1 Wang, 355.
2 Culler, 2.
3 Barthes.
4 Dann, *The Language of Tourism*, 2.
5 Urry & Larsen, *The Tourist Gaze*, 14.
6 Salazar and Graburn, *Tourism Imaginaries*, 1.
7 Infocom, *Zork*.
8 Nitsche, *Video Game Spaces*.
9 Rough Guides, "Introduction," para. 2–3.
10 Tuttle, "Xbox Launches Tourism Campaign for Game Worlds."
11 Bazin, *The Myth of Total Cinema*, 236.
12 Carroll, *Sylvie and Bruno*.
13 Fuller and Jenkins, *Nintendo and New World Travel Writing*.
14 Manovich, *Language of New Media*, 272; Gunkel, *Gaming the System*, 29–30.
15 Murray, *Hamlet on the Holodeck*, 99.
16 Linden Lab, *Second Life*.
17 Castronova, *Exodus to the Virtual World*.
18 Apple, "Introducing Apple Vision Pro," 2023.
19 Newton, "Mark Zuckerberg Is Betting," para. 13.
20 Bilton, "Metaverse."
21 Certeau, *The Practice of Everyday Life*, 117.
22 Helmond et al., "Facebook's Evolution," 124.
23 Csikszentmihalyi, *Flow*, 3–6.
24 Soderman, *Against Flow*, 35.
25 Soderman, *Against Flow*, 5–6.
26 Primack et al., "Use of Multiple Social Media Platforms."
27 Wu et al., "Defining the Determinants."
28 Elliot, "Finding Flow in the Tourist Experience," 107.
29 Coffey & Csikszentmihalyi, "Finding Flow During a Vacation," 80.
30 Van Nuenen, *Scripted Journeys*, 105.
31 In Arthurs & Zacharias, 100.
32 Laughton, *Defective Holiday*.
33 Layman, *Defective Holiday*.
34 Shklovsky, "Art as a Technique."
35 Derrida, *Writing and Difference*, 240.
36 Salen and Zimmerman, *Rules of Play*, 378–87.
37 Gee, "Video Games and Embodiment," 258.
38 Gibson, *Senses*.
39 Huizinga, *Homo Ludens*.
40 Gadamer, *Truth and Method*, 106.

41 Chess, *Play like a Feminist*, 101.
42 See e.g. IGN, "Portal Developers React."
43 Chess, *Play like a Feminist*, 101.
44 Percy, *The Message in the Bottle*, 49.
45 Galloway, *Gaming*, 90–91.
46 Bartle, *Hearts, Clubs, Diamonds, Spades*, 2–3.
47 Hamari and Tuunanen, "Player Types," 29–30.
48 Kagen, *Wandering Games*, 10.
49 These strategies are familiar from 18th and 19th-century travel writing; see e.g. Leask, *Curiosity*, 25.
50 Shklovsky, *Theory of Prose*, 61.

References

Apple. "Introducing Apple Vision Pro: Apple's First Spatial Computer." Apple Newsroom. Last modified June 5, 2023, https://www.apple.com/newsroom/2023/06/introducing-apple-vision-pro/.
Arthurs, Jane, and Usha Zacharias. "Introduction: Digital Games and Gender." *Feminist Media Studies* 7, no. 1 (2007): 97–110, doi:10.1080/14680770601103779.
Barthes, Roland. *Mythologies*. New York: Farrar, Straus & Giroux, 1972.
Bartle, Richard. "Hearts, Clubs, Diamonds, Spades: Players Who Suit Muds." *Journal of MUD Research* 1, no. 1 (1996): 1–19.
Bazin, André. "The Myth of Total Cinema." *What Is Cinema, 2 Volumes*, University of California Press, 1967.
Bilton, Nick. "The Metaverse Is About to Change Everything." Vanity Fair, October 22, 2021, https://www.vanityfair.com/news/2021/10/the-metaverse-is-about-to-change-everything/amp.
Carroll, Lewis. *Sylvie and Bruno*. Project Gutenberg, 2015, http://www.gutenberg.org/files/48630/48630-h/48630-h.htm.
Castronova, Edward. *Exodus to the Virtual World: How Online Fun Is Changing Reality*. New York: St. Martin's Publishing Group, 2007.
Certeau, Michel de. *The Practice of Everyday Life*. Berkeley: University of California Press, 1984.
Chess, Shira. *Play like a Feminist*. Cambridge: MIT Press, 2020.
Coffey, John K., and Mihály Csikszentmihalyi. "Finding Flow During a Vacation." In *The Routledge Handbook of Health Tourism*, edited by Melanie Kay Smith and László Puczkó, 79–88. Abingdon: Routledge, 2016.
Csikszentmihalyi, Mihály. *Flow: The Psychology of Optimal Experience*. New York: Harper Collins, 2009.
Culler, Jonathan. *Framing the Sign: Criticism and Its Institutions*. Norman: University of Oklahoma Press, 1990.
Dann, Graham M.S. *The Language of Tourism: A Sociolinguistic Perspective*. Wallingford: CAB International, 1996.
Derrida, Jacques. *Writing and Difference*. London: Routledge, 2001.
Elliot, Statia. "Finding Flow in the Tourist Experience." In *The Routledge Handbook of the Tourist Experience*, edited by Richard Sharpley, 101–12. London: Routledge, 2022, doi:10.4324/9780429020193.

Fuller, Mary, and Henry Jenkins. "Nintendo and New World Travel Writing: A Dialogue." In *Cybersociety: Computer-Mediated Communication and Community*, edited by S. G. Jones, 57–72. London: Sage, 1995.

Gadamer, Hans Georg. *Truth and Method*. London: Continuum, 2004, doi:10.1007/BF02355429.

Galloway, Alexander R. *Gaming: Essays on Algorithmic Culture*. Minneapolis: University of Minnesota Press, 2006.

Gee, James Paul. "Video Games and Embodiment." *Games and Culture* 3, no. 3–4 (2008): 253–63, doi:10.1177/1555412008317309.

Gibson, James J. *The Senses Considered as Perceptual Systems*. Crows Nest: George Allen & Unwin, 1969, doi:10.2307/3331482.

Guerrilla Games. *Horizon Zero Dawn*. Sony Interactive Entertainment. PlayStation 4. 2017.

Gunkel, David J. *Gaming the System*. Bloomington: Indiana University Press, 2018.

Helmond, Anne, David B. Nieborg, and Fernando N. van der Vlist. "Facebook's Evolution: Development of a Platform-as-Infrastructure." *Internet Histories* 3, no. 2 (2019): 123–46. London: Routledge, doi:10.1080/24701475.2019.1593667.

Huizinga, Johan. *Homo Ludens: Study of the Play-Element in Culture*. New York: Angelico Press, 2016.

Hunicke, Robin. "Designing Future Realities." YouTube, August 2, 2019, https://www.youtube.com/watch?v=l7D5GCV1-kM.

IGN. "Portal Developers React to Multiple Speedruns (Valve Software)." YouTube, October 9, 2021, https://www.youtube.com/watch?v=ZqrmerjGZ14&ab_channel=IGN.

Infocom. *Zork*. Personal Software, Infocom, Activision. PDP-10. 1980.

Kagen, Melissa. *Wandering Games*. Cambridge: MIT Press, 2022.

Kaufman, Eleanor, and Kevin Jon Heller. *Deleuze & Guattari: New Mappings in Politics, Philosophy, and Culture*, edited by Eleanor Kaufman and Kevin Jon Heller. Minneapolis: University of Minnesota Press, 1998.

Laughton, Kim. *Defective Holiday*. Kim Laughton. Microsoft Windows. 2020.

Layman, Eric. "Defective Holiday." Digital Chumps, May 1, 2020, http://digitalchumps.com/defective-holiday-review.

Leask, Nigel. *Curiosity and the Aesthetics of Travel Writing, 1770–1840*. Oxford: Oxford University Press, 2002.

Linden Lab. *Second Life*. Linden Lab. Microsoft Windows. 2003.

Manovich, Lev. *The Language of New Media*. Cambridge: MIT Press, 2001.

Murray, Janet H. *Hamlet on the Holodeck*. Los Angeles: The Free Press, 2016.

Newton, Casey. "Mark Zuckerberg Is Betting Facebook's Future on the Metaverse." *The Verge*, July 22, 2021, https://www.theverge.com/22588022/mark-zuckerberg-facebook-ceo-metaverse-interview.

Nitsche, Michael. *Video Game Spaces: Image, Play, and Structure in 3D Worlds*. Cambridge: MIT Press, 2008.

Percy, Walker. *The Message in the Bottle: How Queer Man Is, How Queer Language Is, and What One Has to Do with the Other*. New York: Farrar, Straus and Giroux, 1975.

Primack, Brian A., Ariel Shensa, César G. Escobar-Viera, Erica L. Barrett, Jaime E. Sidani, Jason B. Colditz, and A. Everette James. "Use of Multiple Social Media Platforms and Symptoms of Depression and Anxiety: A Nationally-Representative

Study among U.S. Young Adults." *Computers in Human Behavior* 69 (2017): 1–9, doi:10.1016/j.chb.2016.11.013.

Rough Guides. "Introduction to the Rough Guide to XBOX." Rough Guides, May 1, 2020, https://www.roughguides.com/articles/introduction-to-the-rough-guide-to-xbox/.

Salazar, Noel B., and Nelson H.H. Graburn, eds. *Tourism Imaginaries: Anthropological Approaches*. New York: Berghahn Books, 2014.

Shklovsky, Viktor. "Art as a Technique." In *Russian Formalist Criticism—Four Essays*, edited by Lee Lemon and Marion Reis, 40–72. Lincoln: University of Nebraska Press, 1965.

Shklovsky, Viktor. *Theory of Prose [O Teorii Prozy]*. Funks Grove: Dalkey Archive Press, 1990.

Soderman, Braxton. *Against Flow: Video Games and the Flowing Subject*. Cambridge: MIT Press, 2021.

Tekinbas, Katie Salen, and Eric Zimmerman. *Rules of Play: Game Design Fundamentals*. Cambridge: MIT Press, 2003.

Tuttle, Will. "Xbox Launches Tourism Campaign for Game Worlds with 'Visit Xbox'." Xbox Wire, April 25, 2019, https://news.xbox.com/en-us/2019/04/25/xbox-launches-tourism-campaign-visit-xbox/.

Tuunanen, Janne, and Juho Hamari. "Meta-synthesis of Player Typologies." In *Proceedings of Nordic Digra 2012 Conference: Games in Culture and Society*, Tampere, Finland, 2012.

Urry, John, and Jonas Larsen. *The Tourist Gaze 3.0*. London: Sage, 2011.

Van Nuenen, Tom. *Scripted Journeys*. Berlin: De Gruyter, 2021.

Wang, Ning. "Rethinking Authenticity in Tourism Experience." *Annals of Tourism Research* 26, no. 2 (1999): 349–70.

Wu, Ing-Long, Mai-Lun Chiu, and Kuei-Wan Chen. "Defining the Determinants of Online Impulse Buying through a Shopping Process of Integrating Perceived Risk, Expectation-Confirmation Model, and Flow Theory Issues." *International Journal of Information Management* 52 (2020): 102099, doi:10.1016/j.ijinfomgt.2020.102099.

Youngs, Tim. "Travel Writing After 1900." In *The Cambridge History of Travel Writing*, edited by Nandini Das and Tim Youngs, 125–39. Cambridge: Cambridge University Press, 2019.

3 King of the Sandbox

The touristic slogan *you can go there* signals scope, awe, and—paradoxically—accessibility. The phrase is most often used in "open-world" or "sandbox" games. These nominators typically refer to a player's freedom of movement and progression in the game's world. My first example here will be the Assassin's Creed series, a franchise of single-player action-adventure games developed primarily by Ubisoft Montreal. Other examples in this genre are series such as Grand Theft Auto,[1] Far Cry,[2] or The Elder Scrolls.[3] I will also discuss *The Legend of Zelda: Breath of the Wild* and *Elden Ring* in order to show how sandbox games can, through very similar mechanics, enable different modalities of gazing.

Gamified History

The Assassin's Creed series takes place in well-known cities and settings during significant historical moments—Rome during the Renaissance, London during the Industrial Revolution, Paris during the French Revolution, and so on. The games generally include recognizable sites that players can visit at their leisure. Assassin's Creed games employ a third-person perspective; you are tasked with taking down targets using your combat and stealth skills. The games integrate science fiction and real-world historical cities and landscapes.

Sandbox games generally consist of many objectives to complete, scattered across the game's map, which can be done at the player's convenience. A significant part of Assassin's Creed's appeal comes from this nonsequential format, couched in the genre of hypertexts and electronic literature that came to rise in the 1990s. Works such as *Patchwork Girl* by Shelley Jackson (1995) use a rhizomatic, multiperspectival structure in which the reader can follow narrative threads in a nonlinear fashion. Lev Manovich has pointed out that this kind of ordering—the ordering of the database—has become the key format for cultural expression in the digital age. What distinguishes the database from the traditional narrative is that they are non-sequentially organized.[4] The imaginary capacity of Assassin's Creed, in other words, is tied to the expectation of plurality, fragmentation, and choice. However, as sandbox

DOI: 10.4324/9781003404590-3

games generally also have a story to tell, they need to reconcile their database structure with the vectors of a linear narrative. In an interview, game designer Amy Hennig discusses this problem of open-world story-based games.

> A story has an author. There's intent behind it. It has a deliberate shape. It has an arc, deliberate landmarks, and a deliberate ending. It gets back to the Aristotelian idea of this ending that's both surprising and inevitable. You can't accidentally do that through a bunch of random events.[5]

It is this tension between the paradigmatic and syntagmatic ordering of player activity I want to explore first. Not so much from a narrative perspective, but because it connects games to a central tension in tourism, between having to follow a guided path, and the fantasy of going off that beaten path. I will argue that one of the ways in which this tension is navigated is in the design of movement through the game world, and the creation of an anti-touristic subject, not unlike the 19th-century flâneur.

The term "sandbox" brings to mind an imaginative transformation of space. A child's sandbox can encompass an entire kingdom, and so can an open-world game. This is clearly how the series is advertised: for instance, the promotional text for *Assassin's Creed Unity*, which takes place in French Revolution-era Paris, reads:

> DISCOVER REVOLUTIONARY PARIS, BROUGHT TO LIFE AS NEVER BEFORE: Carve through the stunning full-scale open world city, a feat only made possible through the power of an all-new game engine.[6]

The promise of a "full scale" city adds significantly to the game's touristic potential. However, while the city's historical landmarks and streets for a large part are represented, the promise remains somewhat of an overstatement. The game makes use of what Michel de Certau depicted as the *asyndeton*: making "gaps in the spatial continuum, retaining only selections or relics from it."[7] The Parisian landmarks—such as the Notre Dame or Bastille—are recreated many times more meticulously than the houses in the city's residential areas, which are there to constitute a patchwork of "Parisianness." Senior level artist Caroline Miousse notably spent two years recreating Notre Dame for *Assassin's Creed Unity*[8] on a near 1:1 scale—a model that became a culturally significant relic as the real building was destroyed by a fire in 2019.

There are also liberties taken in terms of the city's historical veracity. The architecture of *Assassin's Creed: Brotherhood*,[9] for instance, is that of the late 16th-century Baroque period, while the game takes place at the beginning of that same century. The Roman Colosseum in *Assassin's Creed II*,[10] to give another example, has a circular rather than an elliptical shape, as rendering elliptical shadows would have been significantly more difficult.[11] Taking note of these anachronisms and distortions, Douglas Dow argues that, despite its immersive and realistic environments, *Assassin's Creed II* should still be seen as "a simulacrum, a version of the city that purports to be a true representation [ζ] but that presents a false likeness instead."[12]

Yet, of course, "immersion" is a subjective effect as much as a product of "true representation." It is not just about historical veracity, but also about the touristic recognizability of the things you can do and see. One of the series' art directors, Mohamed Gambouz, calls this the "postcard effect."[13] The transformation of historical sites in Assassin's Creed serves to render them immediately recognizable to the series' wide audience. The result is a friction between the archaeological record and the popular imagination of certain places—a phenomenon called *polychronia*.[14] The game negotiates between the site's historical accuracy and its representation through the tourist gaze.

How can we best imagine the condensed grandeur of Assassin's Creed's historical cities? As consumptive spaces, the design ideal for open-world games is the zoo or theme park.[15] Game worlds generally include topographical and ecological variation, with different climates and geo-zones appearing alongside one another. These compressed zones are expressions of the global shrinkage experienced in modernity, discussed by historians such as Wolfgang Schivelbush.[16] In virtualized cities such as those in Assassin's Creed, sites or areas that one might physically pass through and envision as "individual" can become pleasantly contiguous when modeled. The journey between them is considered insignificant and entirely unproblematic.

Indeed, cities in Assassin's Creed are essentialized but fragmented, with tourist hotspots as the main attractions. The games insist on keeping the player's attention diffusely oriented towards many different tasks, through densely filled maps with icons for points of interest, side-quests, and treasures. There is, as in many a tourist exercise, "something to do around every corner." In its presentation of the world as a set of personalized "collectibles," Assassin's Creed brings to mind the markers one leaves on Google Maps.[17] Both emphasize that our touristic relationship with a destination is one of particularized, detailed opportunity (see Figure 3.1).

Beyond these playful forms of mapping, the Assassin's Creed series has begun to implement more explicit forms of touristic navigation. The series is perfectly suited for digitally inspired tourism: for years, there have been "Assassin's Creed pilgrimages" on travel forums such as TripAdvisor, as well as YouTube comparisons between tourist sites as they are rendered both inside the game and outside of it.[18] Photographer Damien Hypolite has produced a series of pictures in which he printed screenshots of *Assassin's Creed Origins*' representation of Paris, and matched them up with their physical counterparts.[19]

The Assassin's Creed developers have in recent years begun to introduce specific game modes to accommodate these kinds of play. The most recent entries in the series include a "Discovery Tour" mode that removes the game's characteristic combat mechanics and instead offers guided tours

34 King of the Sandbox

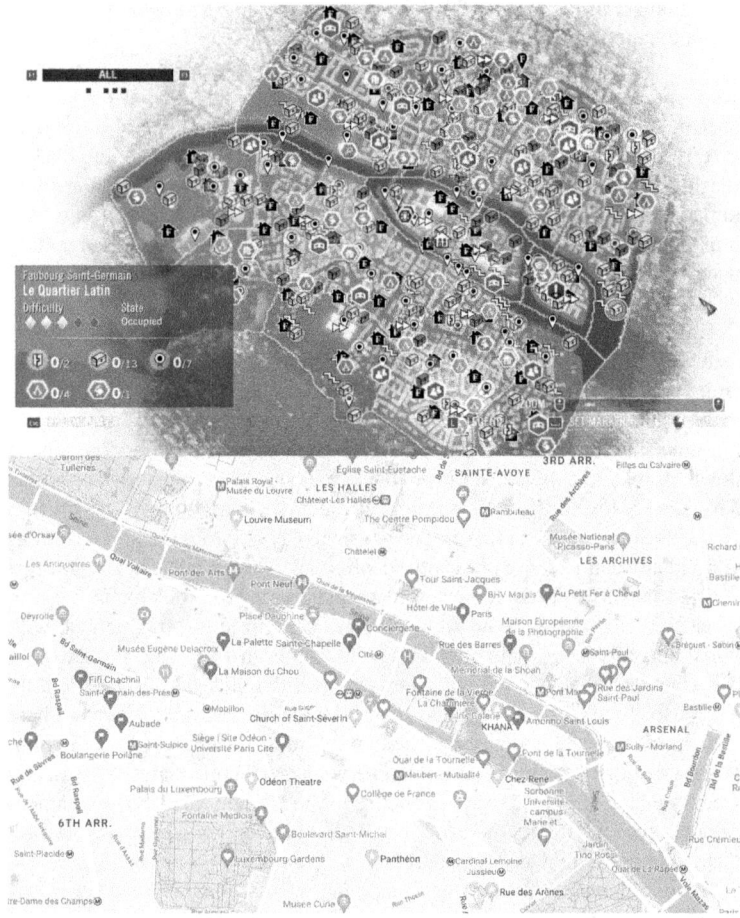

Figure 3.1 Map icons of Paris in *Assassin's Creed Unity* and Google Maps. Author screenshot.

and information on the environment. Some of these tours can be purchased as a standalone package, and they guide novice players through prompts indicating which buttons to push. This is useful, as Triple-A games such as Assassin's Creed typically come with high barriers to entry: both in terms of cost of the game and the platform on which it is played, and in terms of learning the manual dexterity of navigating through 3D space. The Discovery Tour can be thought of as a form of retroactive *degamification*, accommodating the tourist gaze at the expense of fail-states and other ludic feedback mechanisms.

The series' first Discovery Tour was built into *Assassin's Creed Origins*, and allowed players to tour parts of Egypt near the end of the Ptolemaic period. The developers created tours around the game's most famous landmarks, organized like in-game missions that are scattered across the map. The tours include a voiced tour guide, camera movements that highlight details in the environment, and historical images that suspend the gameplay. It is a playground, too: while physical tourists are not legally allowed to climb the Pyramid of Cheops, the Discovery Tour lets players scale the pyramid's lower sections, as well as crawl through smaller tunnels within the structure. These tours are relatively short, ranging from five to twenty minutes (see Figure 3.2).

However, with the release of *Assassin's Creed Valhalla*,[20] the developers reimagined the historical tour as a more dramatized experience. The game's Discovery Tour, which takes place during the time of the Viking raiders, was presented as a movie-length experience that favors immersion over a sense of historical objectivity. Players take on the role of a Viking merchant and sailmaker, a Saxon monk, and Alfred the Great. In its roughly 90-minute story, the game reimagines the Viking age through a dramatic arc, instead of through the kind of objective fact-finding that characterizes most guided museum tours. The developers' aim was to bring players "closer to the material by putting them at the center of it."[21]

For instance, when you take on the role of a young monk, you learn about the history behind the monastic practices they're carrying out. Maxime Durand, the world design director for Discovery Tour, explained the design choice: "empathy leads to learning because we care about the characters, and

Figure 3.2 Discovery Tour in *Assassin's Creed Origins*. Author screenshot.

also doing the things with the character, with the avatar, actually leads also to greater learning and greater comprehension."[22]

As an experiment in virtual tourism, these Discovery Tours are straddling the line between player agency and historical awareness. Sociocultural narratives and immutable events do not easily lend themselves to the free-form manipulation we associate with sandbox gaming. A tourist visiting historical sites is bound by the reality of the past; they can observe, learn, and immerse themselves in a bygone era, but they cannot change it. Tourists and players, in that context, are antonymous. It is the problem of touristic powerlessness that the main mode in Assassin's Creed is responding to as well.

Hiding From the City, In the City

While the Discovery Tour player is a cognizant tourist, the original game engages with touristic questions in more implicit ways. The game also provides what in the literature is sometimes called an anti-touristic sentiment. Anti-tourism, while as old as tourism itself, typically refers to an identity concept that arises amidst the social relations in contemporary mass tourism: it revolves around the desire to be separated from the perceived commonalities of the crowd.[23] It is defined by an aversion to the superficial experiences that are associated with traditional tourism, and can be traced back to the popularization of Rome as a tourist destination during the 18th century. During this time, Romantic writers such as William Wordsworth and George Gordon Byron started explicitly disassociating themselves from what they considered the vulgar forms of experience that accompanied it. This is not to say that the anti-tourist refers to a class that is wholly distinct from the tourist. Instead, the tourist gaze itself is charged with sentiments about distancing oneself from other tourists.[24]

Assassin's Creed primarily enacts the anti-touristic stance through its forms of mobility and perception. Of key importance here is the deployment of the bird's-eye perspective, which brings to mind the top-down overview found in strategy games. The player, to borrow some terms from Sybille Lammes, does not only act out of a mode of "individual experience" but takes on the role of a "cartographer on tour."[25] The dialectics of horizontal and vertical orientations—being in the landscape and overlooking it—is a central feature of Assassin's Creed, consistently implemented since the series' beginnings. You can "claim" certain areas of its cities in an archetypical phallic fashion by climbing to the top of a region's tallest building. Towering above the city results in a panoramic view, distancing players from the city and turning it into an object of pure spatial possibility. As you climb the buildings, the map of the territory is filled with icons, meaning that you can see a new range of activities on their maps that you can undertake.

Having the "world at your feet" is built on the visual language of the overview, and the sense of scope that makes the overview necessary. Tourism scholar Sean Smith calls this language, which is found throughout tourist photography, the "promontory gaze." It is a form of taking possession of a landscape, and a way of looking that "scrubs the landscape of the tourist destination of any sign of human habitation but that of the tourist."[26] The promontory gaze harkens back to Alexander von Humboldt's survey work in Latin America,[27] in which the explorer depicts himself as a small and indomitable figure standing fearless against the epic scale of nature. This visual language was embraced in the paintings of the Romantics, including Caspar David Friedrich's *Wanderer above the Sea of Fog* from Chapter 1. As Smith explains, "The 'promontory' gained by the elevation of the subject's gaze is indicative, at once, of the metaphysical solace delivered by the view as well as alluding to mastery of the scene beheld."

Assassin's Creed players can, when looking over the city, return to the surface through what is perhaps the series' most iconic moment: leaping off a tall building into a conveniently placed haystack. Back on the ground, the series' stealth mechanics form a further means to distinguish player-characters from their surroundings. As the titular assassin, players are required to sneak up on enemies and move through the city undetected: much of the game's *play* consists of breaking into high-security areas and assassinating targets. This is typically followed by an escape sequence in which players evade their pursuers by making use of the city's infrastructure. This can mean climbing on rooftops, hiding in the aforementioned haystacks, or moving surreptitiously among a group of citizens. Locals, insofar as they matter, are part of a nameless crowd whose presence is commensurate to their capacity to assist or stand in the way of the player-character. These dynamics are firmly rooted in the ideology of anti-tourism, which is one of waywardness and *freedom* from touristic structure.[28]

While the assassin is able to blend in with the crowd, they most certainly are not a part of it. The environments in Assassin's Creed are designed to accommodate this power fantasy. The most notable gameplay mechanics in the series involve free running and parkour—a popular sport that makes use of a city's architecture for athletic and explorative running. The game's environments are littered with architectural signifiers: arcades, chimneys, aprons, branches, arches, finger pockets, edges, and balconettes. The player-character in Assassin's Creed also frequently enters iconic churches, cathedrals, and other buildings: in these spaces, a specific parkour path is set out as a type of puzzle, where the player-character has to find out which route to take to the goal. Flow trumps historical accuracy: senior designer Caroline Miousse has explained, for instance, how some liberties had to be taken with item placement in Notre Dame to create paths suitable for parkour.

A tactile dimension also comes into play here, as the free-running gameplay is enabled through certain controller inputs. In Assassin's Creed, pressing down one single button and moving the control stick in the direction one wants to go activates "free run mode," which means the player-character automatically scales buildings, jumps between building roofs or pushes away obstructing onlookers. For the player, it involves a prolonged pull of the right trigger—which is tellingly used in racing games to accelerate, and in first-person shooters to fire the weapon. The input activates an all-purpose mode of locomotion that allows the player-character to continuously thrust forward, and in which the game's architecture stops being an obstacle.

This efficient movement through the city becomes a semi-automated endeavor that requires minimal effort on the player's part. The game's historical tourist sites are traversed by means of a deeply touristic logic—that is, one that involves as few inconveniences or roadblocks as possible, and in which hitting those roadblocks implies only a minimal disruption of flow. Player defeat in Assassin's Creed is equally forgiving: the game employs an auto-save function that ensures players do not have to retry sections they previously completed. Games require a degree of uncertainty to hold our interest, and here the uncertainty is touristic: the main risk, for the player, is the possible breakdown of flow.

The importance of this touristic flow is further underscored by its complete absence in other sections of the game. The framing device for the game's historical tourism is formed by a fictional technological device called the Animus, which allows the game's protagonists to enter a virtual reality constructed from the memories of their ancestors. In *Assassin's Creed*,[29] the current-day protagonist Desmond Miles is kidnapped and forced to relive his ancestors' experiences inside the Animus. While these ancestors move through the middle eastern landscape with ease, Desmond is confined to slogging back and forth from his living quarters to the VR bench in the adjacent room.

The use of VR as a narrative device provides a diegetic reason for the visibility of the player-character's life bar and lit-up target areas, telling them where to go. When you amble too far away from the intended path, the player-character falls "out of sync" with the memories and is forced to try again. In spite of Assassin's Creed's denomination as a sandbox, and in spite of the promontory gaze signaling the player's mastery over the landscape, the game's protagonist cannot change the past, and players can only do their best to adhere to the "tour."

The power they do have is that of self-concealment. A large part of the series' allure derives from the typically modern, urban desire to be separate from the crowds while, paradoxically, hiding among them. The city is a phantasmagoric inventory of images and crowds, and the player becomes a sort of *flâneur*. First envisioned by Charles Baudelaire and later expanded upon by Walter Benjamin, the flâneur is a character associated with the modern, metropolitan lifestyle. He is a masculine-coded figure strolling through and making sense of the cityscape through a kind of totalizing, distanced observation. Initially, flânerie was tied to the socio-cultural atmosphere of Paris in the 19th century—but it quickly became a cipher to grapple with the conditions of (post-)modernity, and a recurring motif in literature, sociology, and art.[30]

Assassin's Creed offers a radicalized flâneur. The player-character is set apart from the virtual crowds by two degrees (a diegetic virtual reality within an extradiegetic virtual reality), and in their sovereign role as "monarch of the crowd"[31] holds a concealed power over life and death itself. The flâneur that is produced here is a highly dysfunctional social element—and perhaps the pinnacle of sociologist Rob Shields' criticism of the flâneur as a "potentially treacherous friend" in a context of excessive individualism "which bypasses social norms in favour of idiosyncratic behaviour."[32] In sum, the thrill that the series offers is not just about the power fantasy of being an assassin. It is the thrill that flânerie enables: taking ownership of a city through concealment. In Charles Baudelaire's famous words: "to see the world, to be at the centre of the world, and yet to remain hidden from the world."[33]

Navigating through the cities of Assassin's Creed fulfills a very similar function as it did for the 19th-century flâneur wandering through Paris: it is a strategy to hide from the alienation that comes with experiencing the overwhelming and threatening modern city. Of course, not every city in Assassin's Creed is modern—the series includes cities from classical antiquity to nineteenth-century London—but what is distinctly modern is their explicit virtuality, both within the game's narrative and to the player. These painstakingly reconstructed digital spaces, as repositories for objectives and side-quests, are meant to overwhelm us. This is why being an assassin is not just a power fantasy, but a coping mechanism in the face of the technological sublime: a way to hide from a meticulously crafted virtual city, in that city.

In some ways, Assassin's Creed also allows us to engage with flânerie as something more than a sign of promontory gazing, excessive individualism, and moral alienation. One can feel insignificant in the city by strolling around in its market squares, parks, or back alleys. These are mundane spaces to take in the atmosphere, to listen to the street noises, and to generally engage in what Melissa Kagen calls wandering: "an activity designed to provoke unproductive, contemplative, anticapitalist play."[34] It is in this way that flânerie can act as a sensibility towards the details and idiosyncrasies of a place, allowing the player's expansionist tourist gaze to be replaced with something more gentle; a form of observation that is not "cut off" from the place, but oriented towards it. Unfortunately, the series' insistence on drama, action, and anti-touristic power makes it hard to engage with it through such an attitude of wandering.

This insistence may be due to a prevailing concern in game design about spaces that are empty and, therefore, "boring." Yet, as Fernando Pessoa once noted, boredom is not the lack of available activity; it is the feeling that there's nothing worth doing. Paradoxically, "this means that the more there is to do, the more tedium one will feel."[35] Pessoa's definition helps us understand why games with an innumerable plentitude of things to complete can still cause ennui. It is in the ambient noises, or the morning light hitting the streets, that Assassin's Creed defamiliarizes its players from the promontory gaze. It is not through monomythical narrative tropes that the sense of stepping back in time is established, but through a sense of the quotidian, and an attentiveness to the minute.

It's All in the Details

We might be tempted to say that the promise of unfettered exploration and focus on environmental size in video games is, by necessity, a colonial echo. But as noted in the previous chapter, we need to be aware of the ways in which games can subvert these expectations. What modes are possible beyond the touristic and anti-touristic modes of Assassin's Creed? It is worth having another look at the game series mentioned in the introduction: The Legend of Zelda.

It might be tempting to describe the series' development throughout the decades as an evolution from simplicity to complexity. All installments of the Zelda series are couched in the technological progress of the medium, including all the affordances of graphics, gameplay, and sound. However, the type of gaze that they encourage has stayed the same: that of the romantic gaze, and of the sublime experience that underlies this gaze. Tourism scholar John Urry described the romantic gaze as a way of consuming sights in which "solitude, privacy and a personal, semi-spiritual relationship with the object of the gaze are emphasized." It is typically projected on "the deserted beach, the empty hilltop, the uninhabited forest, the uncontaminated mountain stream and so on."[36] I am particularly interested in how the Zelda series seeks after a sense of the sublime, while also seeking ways to subvert it.

When we look at the first 3D entry in the series, *The Legend of Zelda: Ocarina of Time* (*OOT*), released in 1998, we see that the game's design is largely prompted by the technical limitations of the Nintendo 64's hardware. The game's map, for instance, has been calculated to span around half a square kilometer. The sense of size and emptiness is maintained through the very limited amount of actionable objects and encounters. In a sense, the high degree of asset recycling, seen in trees, bushes, and walls, as well as the game's monotonous landscapes, only contributes to the game's sense of scope. These spaces seemed large and overwhelming during the early days of 3D modeling, but in retrospect can be considered boring for the very same reasons. Compared to the bustling sites of Assassin's Creed, walking through Hyrule Field, the game's central hub, feels distinctly uneventful.

The move to the third dimension also marks the beginning of extensive touristic guidance in the series. Like Assassin's Creed, the Zelda games have developed practices to aid their players in navigating their games' spatial narrative, commonly filed under the name of "hand-holding." In *OOT*, the player is led from goal to goal through copious advice. The game has since become somewhat renowned for these practices. It is easy to draw comparisons to the 1986 NES game, which famously set the player free in the world without any narrative cues. One result of *OOT*'s hand-holding is a tension between player-initiated *exploration* of its space, the series' original approach to mobility through intrinsic motivation, and its restriction by *navigation*, in which the player is guided and assisted by the game. The many concerned cries of Link's companion in *OOT*, Navi—her very name referring to her function as navigator—have been an object of ridicule among player communities since the early 2000s. The solitary romantic gaze was in conflict with the game's heavily assisted navigation.

In 2017, Nintendo radically adjusted the structure of its Zelda series. *The Legend of Zelda: Breath of the Wild (BOTW)*[37] offered a surprisingly different type of experience than its direct predecessors through its sandbox structure, reminiscent of Assassin's Creed and similar games. The game's map now counted around 61 square kilometers, about the size of Kyoto.[38] The game's different biomes were openly accessible to players, and the assisted navigation of earlier titles was replaced by a range of familiar panoptic practices. This is established from the game's opening: as Link walks outside, the camera zooms past bushes and over a cliffside, offering an overview of the world and its towering landmarks (see Figure 1.3).

The moment encapsulates the game's touristic promise of opportunity. As I noted in Chapter 1, it draws heavily on the romantic imagery of Caspar David Friedrich (see Figure 1.4), and the era's reverence for the sublime, the individual, and the interplay of man with nature. However, in Friedrich's painting, the sublime is largely signaled by the fog, which obscures parts of the landscape and causes a sense of unease and uncertainty. *BOTW* does not obscure anything; instead, it triggers the sublime through the overwhelming magnitude of the virtual landscape at the player-character's feet. One of the main modes of transportation is a paraglider, allowing the player-character to sail over the landscape after climbing to a high point. The gaze, in *BOTW*, is related to opportunity: most places that can be seen can be reached by gliding over. In sum, *BOTW*'s landscape is clearly organized around the promontory gaze.

This sense of mastery over the landscape connects the game to the colonial histories I have been discussing. Though developed by a Japanese company, Zelda's storyline is marked by a distinctly Western genealogy—it involves a hero's journey prompted by a divine call, an Arthurian sword lodged in stone, and a stark contrast between good and evil. This leads to an approach to space that openly invites postcolonial readings. Ricardo Quintana Vallejo, for instance, notes that:

> *Breath of the Wild* is a metaphor of European Colonialism. The main character, a white, blue-eyed young man is *destined* to save the world. [...] Link has the burden to visit the most *exotic* and wild places of the planet because the inhabitants need him to save them."[39]

Indeed, in this sense, *BOTW* is firmly rooted in a colonial dream. It cultivates the promontory gaze as players climb scattered towers in order to survey the landscape and update their map. However, *BOTW* crucially does not provide the icons on that map. The main advantage of having an overview is that players themselves can see and mark the sights that look interesting to explore. This, I would argue, is more than a variation on the same colonial theme ("*you* pick which places you want to discover and save"). It allows for a less "productive" kind of wandering in the game world. The European cover art of *BOTW*, which differs from its American counterpart, bears this out.

The European cover features a distinctly more colorful and friendly color palette. Link is on a patch of grass instead of a big rock, looking over his shoulder at the camera. He comes off less like Friedrich's anonymous wanderer, and more like he is taking a tourist selfie during a stroll through the mountains (see Figure 3.3).

It is through this ethos of meandering that *BOTW* complicates its own colonial gaze. Players are asked to be attentive to details and are nudged towards serendipitous diversion. *BOTW* does not simply aim to overwhelm: it asks a more gentle question about what there is to do in the first place. The

Figure 3.3 Cover art for EU and US versions of *The Legend of Zelda: Breath of the Wild.* Author screenshot.

player's relationship to the landscape is not so much one of mastery but of detail-oriented curiosity, in which minute encounters and landmarks are littered throughout the landscape.

This curiosity openly clashes with the game's monomythical narrative. Though *BOTW* adopts the epic Arthurian story of saving the world by divine mandate, that structure stands in sharp contrast with the kind of frivolous loitering that makes up most of the actual game. There's a productive ludo-narrative tension that makes you wonder whether some detail or small encounter isn't *just as interesting* as the grand mission.

We are once again reminded of the flâneur, to whom observing and looking are of a dispersed and transitory nature.[40] However, the flânerie present in *BOTW* does not call to mind Rob Shields' "potentially treacherous friend," but rather embeds the game in the tradition of digressive literature, such as Laurence Sterne's *The Life and Opinions of Tristram Shandy, Gentleman* (1759–1767). The book often moves away from the main storyline to introduce new characters, anecdotes, and observations, and Sterne's narrator frequently goes off on tangents, interrupting the narrative flow with lengthy discussions on a variety of subjects. Viktor Shklovsky wrote that these forms of "poetic disorder" are, at their core, defamiliarizing.[41] I would argue that a similar quaintness characterizes Link's meanderings through Hyrule: instead of saving the world, he is out to catch a fish, find a Korok, or find an ingredient for an NPC who wants to make curry rice.

While these diversions are comedic, they also have an aesthetic dimension. The sublime is secondary to the game's sense of "poetic realism." The 19th-century literary movement disregarded overwhelming and cataclysmic events, instead focusing on everyday experiences. The approach is captured by Adalbert Stifter's "law of the gentle": the quiet, gentle forces that work over long periods of time. In his novella *Rock Crystal*, Stifter contrasts the violence of a snowstorm with the persistent and gentle effects of weathering that form a glacier.[42]

Some of these small-scale encounters involve Korok spirits that you can find throughout the map: friendly creatures who, upon being found, give you a small reward. There are no less than 900 Koroks, although the game crucially does not explicitly count them. The joy of finding out these creatures is partly due to the fact that these seeds can be redeemed for upgrades, but importantly, there is an autotelic reason for doing so as well. Koroks are found through solving environmental puzzles, such as following a trail of flowers or placing a rock in a consciously incomplete rock formation.

The ubiquity of minor encounters creates a constant state of diversion, where the player is encouraged to forget the overall mission in favor of detail-oriented excursions. *BOTW* emphasizes the social emptiness of the world through its relative scarcity of non-player characters and encounters, as well as its minimalist soundtrack which sharply differs from the orchestral grandeur found throughout the series. In terms of environmental oddities, however, the game world is quite dense. There is an antecedent of these serendipitous discoveries in prior entries in the series, where out-of-place rocks or cracks in the wall signified hidden treasures. Their ubiquity in *BOTW*, however, causes a subversion of the tourist gaze, which moves from a macroscopic scale pointed at mountains, gorges, and horizons, to a microscopic scale.

The focus on curiosity is one of the ways in which *BOTW* inserts itself into a discursive tradition of Japanese aesthetic philosophy. It also highlights the transient, fleeting beauty of the world, with ruins scattered throughout the game's world, and the game's understated piano-led soundtrack hinting at a sense of sadness and nostalgia. Though a proper cultural analysis of Japanese concepts such as "mono no aware"[43] go beyond the scope of this chapter, summarizing *BOTW* as an occidental power fantasy alone ignores the clear and persistent semiotics of impermanence that the game expresses.

An example of my own playthrough may clarify how this ethos of minutia and impermanence promotes a different type of gazing. I was steering Link around on a horse when a few stray piano notes started playing in the background. The notes stood out as the game is often silent, favoring the ambient sound effects of nature. I first felt the music had to signify something contextual, some secret I missed. I dismounted and started exploring my surroundings, but the music stopped. Later, I learned that the song would only play as I rode on. When the violin joined in, I found myself listening to a very understated rendition of the game's classic theme song. The song, typically rendered in the series as a bombastic anthem, had been reduced to another detail, dependent on a fleeting mode of transportation. The player of *BOTW* needs to engage with the surroundings with an open mind and attentive ear, letting the environment itself provide direction and guidance rather than barreling through it en route to accomplish a mission.

The moment provides an alternative perspective on how we interact with our surroundings during travel. Tying music to particular activities, instead of places, challenges our propensity to categorize and compartmentalize experiences. Our tourist gaze—so often fixated on a point on our map, or on what is on the horizon—can be punctuated by unexpected exchanges or intricacies that do not necessarily conform to the journey's broader narrative. This means more than the usual mantra of "it's the journey, not the destination." It subtly invites us to reconsider the relationship between our actions and the environment.

In sum, both *BOTW* and the Assassin's Creed series enable the kind of flow that characterizes the frictionless touristic enterprise, and both are organized along the lines of the promontory gaze. But there is an important difference between the litany of control and oversight, and the diversion from oversight by detail and a sense of transience. My point is this: while the tourist gaze is easily mobilized as a form of regulatory, stabilizing power, it can also be conceived as something that is itself in motion. The expectation of a stable semiotic anchor can be subverted by types of gazing that are destabilizing and unsettling, and that thereby allow for a reflection on one's transient touristic status.

A Meaningless Overview

For a final example of how the promontory gaze can be subverted, consider *Elden Ring*,[44] a dark fantasy action role-playing game that has much in common with *BOTW*. Both games are action role-playing games, played in a third-person perspective, with gameplay focusing on combat and exploration. In both games, you explore an open world, unlocking new sections of the map as they progress. However, like the Dark Souls series that developer FromSoftware released before it, *Elden Ring* asks more of the player than *BOTW*—both in terms of manual dexterity and interpretative skill.

Like previous FromSoftware's titles, *Elden Ring* is a notably difficult game. That is to say, players can expect to die and have to repeat a battle many times. Hidetaka Miyazaki, the game's director, told *The New Yorker* upon the game's release about his design goal: "to experience the joy that comes from overcoming hardship."[45] That hardship does not only pertain to the combat; the game is also purposefully obscure and disorienting in terms of its storytelling and layout. *Elden Ring's* narrative is delivered through cryptic dialogue with non-player characters, item descriptions, and *environmental storytelling*, which conveys a story through the context and details of a setting, rather than relying on explicit dialogue or text. You are prompted to actively explore and interpret the environment, piecing together the narrative from subtle clues—for instance, a shattered statue near a ruined castle hints at a long-forgotten battle against an ancient foe.

Elden Ring's popularity can be explained by the fusion of this kind of opaque storytelling and the opacity of the world itself. You are deciphering a landscape that remains, in many ways, indifferent to their presence. Enemies that you might have waged long, drawn-out battles against respawn as soon as you reach a checkpoint. There's also barely any sense of altitude in the game, and there are only a few moments where you can reach high ground to survey their surroundings, as is common in the genre. Even then, the world of *Elden Ring* feels decidedly unnatural and dreamlike: mountains do not look like mountains, and water is either ankle-shallow or too deep to survive.

Mapping is similarly disconnected from its colonialist roots. Players need to encounter map fragments in order to see a more detailed outline of the part of the world they are traveling through. Like in *BOTW*, however, this map is notably scarce in terms of icons—opposite to the information-dense iconography in Assassin's Creed (see Figure 2.2). The game leaves it up to the player to place their own markers to denote places they have visited or that look interesting on the map. Yet in *Elden Ring*, this capacity is not necessarily tied to a sense of agency. This is largely due to the imperviousness of *Elden Ring*'s landscape, which is designed to be actively intimidating. The game makes a concentrated effort to hide most of its world: there are a plethora of portals to hidden places, and the game features a daunting amount of hidden caves and ruins. There is also an entire underground realm that is only exposed when the player happens on an elevator in the overworld.

This misleading sense of scale is also realized by defamiliarizing common features of the landscape. Take for instance the large golden trees that you see in the distance as you begin to explore the world. These are much larger than they might seem to be, meaning that traveling to them takes much longer than one might think. To make matters yet more confusing, *Elden Ring* lacks a quest log, typical for the sandbox genre, meaning players are not able to check which tasks and quests still need to be completed. It is hard to recall where you have been, or where you are going. In the few moments that the game does offer an overview of the landscape, the view is, paradoxically, disorienting and unsettling. Contrary to a game like *BOTW*, having an overview does not mean a place is immediately accessible, as the player-character has no means of navigating the landscape by air. What also stands out is the fog covering the landscape—more clearly taking a cue from Friedrich's painting than *BOTW*. The overview offers nothing more than some vague clues about what awaits you (see Figure 3.4).

Because *Elden Ring* refuses to offer a helpful overview, the player remains embedded in the chaos of the scenery. The effect, more than in the other games mentioned so far, is that the player feels lost in the world. The touristic experience is not one of potentiality through a sense of power but through its opposite. It is not about the promise that *you can go there*, but about asking,

Figure 3.4 A disorienting overview in *Elden Ring*. Author screenshot.

where the hell am I? The game's main figure of speech is continuous addition: even when you think you have an overview, wresting a sense of control from the environment, another whole area is revealed. The player constantly has to revise their view on the totality they are facing.

In this sense, *Elden Ring* radicalizes a form of trickery that all open-world games engage in. The game is impressive because it seems endless, as though there is always one more thing preventing the gaze from completion. However, the inevitable result of this mirage is the sense of loss or anticlimax that surfaces at that moment when the landscape has finally been exhausted—the moment when the player realizes they have seen all the sites and become fully familiar with the world, and thereby robbed it of an essential part of its appeal. All virtual sandboxes have this in common: they hold our attention and confine us to the magic circle of play because some part of them remains unexplored. In the next chapters, I want to discuss some alternatives to this consumptive logic of tourism.

Notes

1. E.g. Rockstar North. *Grand Theft Auto V*.
2. E.g. Ubisoft Toronto, *Far Cry 6*.
3. E.g. Bethesda Game Studios, *The Elder Scrolls V: Skyrim*.
4. Manovich, *Database as Symbolic Form*, 80.
5. In Takahashi, para. 93.
6. Ubisoft Montreal, *Assassin's Creed Unity*.
7. Certeau, Practices of Space, 37.
8. Ubisoft Montreal, *Assassin's Creed Unity*.
9. Ubisoft Montreal, *Assassin's Creed: Brotherhood*.
10. Ubisoft Montreal, *Assassin's Creed II*.
11. Hsu, "Renaissance Scholar."
12. Dow, "Historical Veneers," 219.
13. Webster, "Building a Better Paris."
14. Westland and Hedlund, "Polychronia."
15. Aarseth, "A Hollow World."
16. Schivelbush, *The Railway Journey*, 38.
17. Google, *Google Maps*.
18. Assassin's Creed Univers, "Game vs Reality."
19. Lee, "Damien Hypolite."
20. Ubisoft Montreal, *Assassin's Creed Valhalla*.
21. Reparaz, "Assassin's Creed Discovery Tour."
22. Wald, ""Discovery Tour."
23. See for instance Buzard, *The Beaten Track*.
24. Dann, "Writing out the Tourist."
25. Lammes, "Spatial Regimes," 267.
26. Smith, "Instagram Abroad," 17.
27. Pratt, *Imperial Eyes*, 120.
28. Week, "I Am Not a Tourist," 195.
29. Ubisoft Montreal, *Assassin's Creed*.
30. Tester, "Introduction," 1.
31. Tester, "Introduction," 4.
32. Shields, "Fancy footwork," 71.

33 Baudelaire, "The Painter of Modern Life," 9.
34 Kagen, *Wandering Games*, 12.
35 Pessoa, *The Book of Disquiet*, 365.
36 Urry and Larsen, *The Tourist Gaze*, 19.
37 Nintendo EPD. *The Legend of Zelda: Breath of the Wild*.
38 Webster, "*Breath of the Wild*'s map is based on Kyoto."
39 Quintana Vallejo, "Breath of the Wild European Colonialism," para. 7.
40 Van Leeuwen, "If we are Flâneurs," 301.
41 Shklovsky, "Sterne's *Tristam Shandy*: Stylistic Commentary," 76.
42 Stifler, *Rock Crystal*.
43 Meli, "Motoori Norinaga's Hermeneutic," 60.
44 FromSoftware, *Elden Ring*.
45 Parkin, "Hidetaka Miyazaki," para 6.

References

Aarseth, Espen J. "A Hollow World: *World of Warcaft* as Spatial Practice." In *Digital Culture, Play, and Identity: A World of Warcraft Reader*, edited by Hilde G. Corneliussen and Jill Walker Rettberg, 111–22. Cambridge: MIT Press, 2008.

Assassin's Creed Univers. "Assassin's Creed Unity – GAME vs REALITY [HD]." YouTube, September 22, 2014, https://www.youtube.com/watch?v=EaA7i8C9194.

Baudelaire, Charles. "The Painter of Modern Life." Translated and edited by J. Mayne. In *Baudelaire CH The Painter of Modern Life and Other Essays*, 1–41. London: Phaidon, 1995 [1863].

Bethesda Game Studios. *The Elder Scrolls V: Skyrim*. Bethesda Softworks. Microsoft Windows. 2011.

Bogost, Ian. *How to Think About Videogames*. Minneapolis: University of Minnesota Press, 2015.

Buzard, J. *The Beaten Track: European Tourism, Literature, and the Ways to Culture, 1800–1918*. Oxford: Oxford University Press, 1993.

Certeau, Michel de. "Practices of Space." In *On Signs*, edited by Marshall Blonsky, 122–45. Baltimore: Johns Hopkins University Press, 1985.

Dann, Graham M. S. "Writing Out the Tourist in Space and Time." *Annals of Tourism Research* 26, no. 1 (January 1999): 159–87, doi:10.1016/S0160-7383(98)00076-0.

DICE. *Mirror's Edge*. Electronic Arts. PlayStation 3. 2008.

Dow, Douglas N. "Historical Veneers: Anachronism, Simulation and Art History in *Assassin's Creed* II." In *Playing with the Past: Digital Games and the Simulation of History*, edited by Matthew Wilhelm Kapell and Andrew B.R. Elliott, 215–32. London: Bloomsbury, 2013.

FromSoftware. *Elden Ring*. Bandai Namco Entertainment. Microsoft Windows. 2022.

Google. *Google Maps*. Accessed June 10, 2023, https://www.google.com/maps.

Hills-Duty, Rebecca. "National Museum of Finland Offers Virtual Time Travel." *VR Focus*, February 16, 2018, https://www.vrfocus.com/2018/02/national-museum-of-finland-offers-virtual-time-travel/.

Hsu, Jeremy. "A Renaissance Scholar Helps Build Virtual Rome." *LiveScience*, November 12, 2010, https://www.livescience.com/8945-renaissance-scholar-helps-build-virtual-rome.html.

Kagen, Melissa. *Wandering Games*. Cambridge: MIT Press, 2022.

Lammes, Sybille. "Spatial Regimes of the Digital Playground: Cultural Functions of Spatial Practices in Computer Games." *Space and Culture* 11, no. 3 (2008): 260–72, doi:10.1177/1206331208319150.

Lee, Kevin. "Damien Hypolite Matches Assassin's Creed Unity's 1789 Paris With 2014 Paris." *ThePhoblographer*, December 21, 2014, https://www.thephoblographer.com/2014/12/11/damien-hypolite-matches-assassins-creed-unitys-1789-paris-2014-paris/.

Manovich, Lev. "Database as Symbolic Form." *Convergence* 5, no. 2 (1999): 80–99, doi:10.1177/135485659900500206.

Meli, Mark. "Motoori Norinaga's Hermeneutic of Mono no Aware: The Link between Ideal and Tradition." In *Japanese Hermeneutics: Current Debates on Aesthetics and Interpretation*, edited by Michael F. Marra, 60–75. Honolulu: University of Hawaii Press, 2002, doi:10.1515/9780824863104-009.

Mukherjee, Souvik. *Videogames and Postcolonialism: Empire Plays Back*. London: Palgrave MacMillan, 2017.

Nintendo EPD. *The Legend of Zelda: Breath of the Wild*. Nintendo. Nintendo Switch. 2017.

Parkin, Simon. "Hidetaka Miyazaki Sees Death as a Feature, Not a Bug." *The New Yorker*, February 25, 2022, https://www.newyorker.com/culture/persons-of-interest/hidetaka-miyazaki-sees-death-as-a-feature-not-a-bug.

Pessoa, Fernando. *The Book of Disquiet*, edited by Richard Zenith. London: Penguin, 2002.

Pratt, Mary Louise. *Imperial Eyes: Travel Writing and Transculturation*. London: Routledge, 1992.

Quintana Vallejo, Ricardo. "The Legend of Zelda: Breath of the Wild European Colonialism and Why We Need to Take Games Seriously." *Terse Journal*, September 12, 2017, https://tersejournal.com/2017/08/12/the-legend-of-zelda-breath-of-the-wild-european-colonialism-and-why-we-need-to-take-games-seriously/.

Reparaz, Mikel. "Assassin's Creed Discovery Tour: Viking Age Launches on October 19." *Ubisoft.com*, September 14, 2021. Accessed June 1, 2023, https://news.ubisoft.com/en-ca/article/fF7Gs9UBA758GopurfZWb/assassins-creed-discovery-tour-viking-age-launches-on-october-19.

Rockstar North. *Grand Theft Auto V*. Rockstar Games. PlayStation 3. 2013.

Schivelbush, Wolfgang. *The Railway Journey*. Berkeley: University of California Press, 2014.

Shields, Rob. "Fancy Footwork." In *The Flâneur*, edited by Keith Tester, 61–80. London: Routledge, 1994.

Shklovsky, Viktor. "Sterne's *Tristam Shandy*: Stylistic Commentary." In *Russian Formalist Criticism—Four Essays*, edited by Lee Lemon and Marion Reis, 40–72. Lincoln: University of Nebraska Press, 1965.

Smith, Sean P. "Instagram Abroad: Performance, Consumption and Colonial Narrative in Tourism." *Postcolonial Studies* 21, no. 2 (2018): 172–91, doi:10.1080/13688790.2018.1461173.

Stifler, Adalbert. *Rock Crystal*. New York: New York Review Books Classics, 2008.

Takahashi, Dean. "Amy Hennig Interview—Surviving the Trauma of Making a Video Game and Inspiring Newcomers." *VentureBeat*, February 22, 2019, https://venturebeat.com/2019/02/22/amy-hennig-interview-surviving-the-trauma-of-making-a-video-game-and-inspiring-newcomers/view-all/.

Tester, Keith. "Introduction." In *The Flâneur*, edited by Keith Tester, 1–21. London: Routledge, 1994.
Ubisoft Montreal. *Assassin's Creed*. Ubisoft. PlayStation 3. 2007.
Ubisoft Montreal. *Assassin's Creed II*. Ubisoft. PlayStation 3. 2009.
Ubisoft Montreal. *Assassin's Creed: Brotherhood*. Ubisoft. PlayStation 3. 2010.
Ubisoft Montreal. *Assassin's Creed Unity*. Ubisoft. Microsoft Windows. 2014.
Ubisoft Montreal. *Assassin's Creed Origins*. Ubisoft. Microsoft Windows. 2017.
Ubisoft Montreal. *Assassin's Creed Valhalla*. Ubisoft. Microsoft Windows. 2020.
Ubisoft Toronto. *Far Cry 6*. Ubisoft. Microsoft Windows. 2021.
Urry, John, and Jonas Larsen. *The Tourist Gaze 3.0*. London: Sage, 2011.
van Leeuwen, Bart. "If we are Flâneurs, Can we be Cosmopolitans?" *Urban Studies* 56, no. 2 (2019): 301–16, doi:10.1177/0042098017724120.
Wald, Heather. "Discovery Tour: Viking Age is a Fantastic Way to Immerse Yourself in the History of Assassin's Creed Valhalla." *Gamesradar*, August 23, 2022, https://www.gamesradar.com/assassins-creed-valhalla-discovery-tour-viking-age/.
Webster, Andrew. *"The Legend of Zelda: Breath of the Wild's* Map Is Based on Kyoto." *The Verge*, March 6, 2017, https://www.theverge.com/2017/3/6/14827832/the-legend-of-zelda-breath-of-the-wild-map-kyoto-japan.
Webster, Andrew. "Building a Better Paris in *Assassin's Creed* Unity." *The Verge*, April 17, 2019, https://www.theverge.com/2014/10/31/7132587/assassins-creed-unity-paris.
Week, Lara. "'I Am Not a Tourist: Aims and Implications of 'Traveling.'" *Tourist Studies* 12 (2012): 186–203, doi:10.1177/1468797612454627.
Westland, Jonathan, and Ragnar Hedlund. "Polychronia—Negotiating the Popular Representation of a Common Past in *Assassin's Creed*." *Journal of Gaming & Virtual Worlds* 8, no. 1 (2016): 3–20.
Whitaker, Bob. "Interview with Maxime Durand on *Assassin's Creed*: Origins and Discovery Tour Mode." *History Respawned*, October 16, 2017, https://www.gamedeveloper.com/console/interview-with-maxime-durand-on-assassin-s-creed-origins-and-discovery-tour-mode.

4 Bigger on the Inside

In the previous chapter, I discussed games that are typical of the modern sandbox genre. These games function in a similar way to theme parks, in that they are both *open* and *compressed*. They can be traversed at will, and are saturated with sights, events, and encounters. The difference is that, compared with theme parks, they can be more expansive, and traversed in more spectacular ways. As such, game designers in this genre develop spaces that are sprawling and awe-inspiring—think back on the overview players are given in the Assassin's Creed series or *The Legend of Zelda: Breath of the Wild (BOTW)*—and that allow players to imagine destinations as sites for possession and consumption. At the same time, designers do well to excise those aspects of travel that are generally considered uneventful or boring. They scale down and prune the cities, villages, mountains, and planets they create in order to minimize the tedium we must deal with on physical trips. The two games I have discussed try to balance a sense of realism (it still *looks* like a city, or a mountain) with a sense of idealism, capturing the touristic essence of a place much like a theme park would.

In the following chapters, I want to discuss games that play around with these dynamics of expansion and compression in other ways. The first genre that comes to mind is sometimes derisively called the *walking simulator*—the gag being that all these games do is simulate a boring pedestrian effort without a proper challenge. Of course, that's a fairly reductive characterization. While the walking sim features little to no combat, and as such is not as taxing in terms of manual dexterity, its embrace of pedestrian movement foregrounds walking as an aesthetic, dramaturgical practice.[1] As games scholar Melissa Kagen argues, the term has become a catch-all for games that take an interest in "alternative modes of expression, embodiment, environment, orientation, and community."[2]

In walking sims, *play* comes to mean something other than the idea of exploration and rational goal-chasing found in the sandbox games of Chapter 3. Walking sims are linear affairs in which the player has little choice about where to go. This sense of strong authorial intent, Jesper Juul says, exemplifies a conservative aesthetics of art. Walking sims, he notes, are "video games that can fit in art gallery settings."[3] It's telling that Miyamoto,

DOI: 10.4324/9781003404590-4

the lead designer of the Legend of Zelda series, does not consider his games works of art, noting in an interview that he prefers to call his games "products," rather than works of art.[4] Walking sims do the opposite, Juul argues: they are not about improving skills or creatively improvising. Instead, they remove challenge in order for the player to approach the work in a more poetic way. As such, they have something in common with visiting a museum: your movement is considerate, slow, contemplative, and observant. But that is not to say there is no "play" in this genre, as is sometimes suggested.

Play has often been defined in terms of the constraints that enable it. Derrida wrote of play—sometimes translated as "freeplay"—as a kind of looseness: "by orienting and organizing the coherence of the system, the center of a structure permits the freeplay of its elements inside the total form."[5] A string not pulled taut has play. Game designers Salen and Zimmerman similarly define play as emerging "both because of and in opposition to more rigid structures."[6]

One question we could ask, then, is whether a higher degree of rigidity simply decreases the amount of play. This is what the criticism of walking sims often amounts to: they are very linear, their dramaturgical elements are meticulously set up, and walking through them is not as much a matter of play as it is of simply observing these elements. Indeed, walking sims are not about strategic optimization, but about playing obediently, *playing with the grain*, letting yourself be taken in by the atmosphere of a place. If there is work to be done, it is a semiotic type of work to make sense of the *mise-en-scène*—the arrangement of scenery and stage properties in front of the player.

This rigidity is both what connects the walking sim to the structures of tourism, and what allows it to defamiliarize the player towards these structures. I will argue that, because the spaces in walking sims are so clearly metonymic, they allow the player to reflect on their touristic intuition to follow a preset experiential script. There is friction as the scale and the constraints of the game's possibility space are scanned and queried.

Touring the Walking Sim

In 2007, Dan Pinbeck, the Creative Director at game company thechineseroom, was funded to develop modifications for popular first-person shooters (FPS) such as *Half-Life 2*. The goal of his research experiment was to distort and manipulate the FPS genre in order to expose and alter the "underlying politics of the game."[7] *Dear Esther*[8] was one of the results of this experiment. Modding out the possibility of killing non-player characters, all that was retained from the genre was the ability to explore a setting from a first-person perspective. Setting the game on an abandoned island in the Hebrides, Scotland, you spend your time listening to a troubled man read a series of letters to his deceased wife. *Dear Esther* was released as a standalone game in 2012. It has had a decisive influence on other games and the "affective landscape experience,"[9] which is characterized by the connections between architecture, landscape, and game design. Game designer Christopher W. Totten calls the act of creating such a virtual world "placemaking."[10] He describes that such "homely places should feature natural or rich materials: grass, wood, brick, stone."[11]

Across the 2010s, a range of games have followed in *Dear Esther's* wake, setting players in natural or homely settings: exemplars are *Gone Home*,[12] *Firewatch*,[13] and *What Remains of Edith Finch*,[14] all of which were released in the last decade and make use of the increasing graphical fidelity of the medium. It is not a coincidence that walking sims became popular at a point when games began approaching photorealism: the fidelity is necessitated by the type of gazing that the walking sim encourages in its players. While we saw in the last chapter how Assassin's Creed encoded a neocolonialist gaze of the cityscape, walking sims offer a different hermeneutic challenge: the player tries to put together a story through the cues and clues they are given. A common method of constructing a narrative in the walking sim, discussed in the last chapter as well, is environmental storytelling: the selection and arrangement of objects players encounter in a game world, so that they suggest a story. Audio logs, letters, ashtrays, teddy bears, and puddles of blood alike can carry referential meaning, acting as non-verbal semiotic signs for players to assemble into a coherent whole.

For instance, in *Gone Home*, you play a 21-year-old American woman returning home from a year overseas to her family home, but finding the house to be abandoned. With few clues as to what's going on, you make your way inside. The game consists of milling through the house's rooms, looking at notes and family portraits, listening to voicemails, and reading the journal of your sister in order to make sense of what has happened in your absence. Environmental storytelling grounds a game within its own fiction through spatial means, and in walking sims, this often consists of "[pursuing] a secret through objects that resonate the ghosts of the past, found in old diaries and discarded letters."[15] Tracing relations between found objects to uncover a story may at first glance seem to connect the walking sim primarily to the detective novel. But this semiotic vigilance connects the walking sim to a broader history of both art and tourism.

As Rebecca Solnit has written, "choosing to walk in the landscape as a contemplative, spiritual, or aesthetic experience has a specific cultural ancestry."[16] I am thinking not so much about the Romantic wandering discussed in Chapter 3, but about the early 20th century, in which the Surrealists began to imagine walking as an aesthetic practice, focusing on chance encounters and irrational meetings to inspire their art. Some decades later, the Situationist International movement explored the *dérive*, a type of unplanned walk in which, as its leading theorist Guy Debord put it, you're drawn in by the "psychogeographical effects" of a place by passing through the "attractions of the terrain and the encounters [you] find there."[17]

What a walking sim does is lay out a meticulous display of attractions and encounters. In *Firewatch*, for instance, you play a fire lookout named Henry, a man running away from his life and his relationship who just began working in Shoshone National Forest. His confession in the game's beginning—"I came out here for a breath of fresh air and some adventure"—is indicative of the escapism that the Wyoming park represents. While the player-character gets to hike through the beautiful environment, Henry's lingering issues come back to haunt him. Strange messages, events, and encounters—the evening light hitting the trees, the silence of the natural environment—it all leads to an increasing sense of dread and paranoia. Henry, and the players with him, edge closer to a sense of mystery, tragedy, and conspiracy about what is going on in the park. The game then ends on an explicitly disappointing note: none of the mysteries turn out to be real. There is catharsis, though, as the game ends in an all-enveloping forest fire that Henry needs to escape from. The park was only a temporary escape from his problems.

Another thing that must be noted is, again, the compression of space that enables the kind of linear storytelling walking sims are known for. Walking sims are not about the expansiveness and scope emphasized by the games in the last chapter. The dominant stylistic device within the rhetoric of spatial practice that the walking sim provides is that of the synecdoche: a relatively small area stands for a narrative totality. In a review for *Firewatch*, *The Guardian* noted how it "is a relatively small game that projects itself big."[18] The forest is not modeled in its entirety, because that is not the game's point. The point is to tease out the mental vulnerabilities of the protagonist whose body you inhabit. The game's wilderness visually and narratively envelopes the player-character: as he explores the forest, Henry engages in walkie-talkie conversations with his supervisor Delilah, and the player gets to know both of these characters in the process (see Figure 4.1).

Like *Gone Home*, *Firewatch* involves spaces that are narratively marked by hardship, crisis, trauma, or death. Walking sims, in other words, do not only use small spaces to represent larger territories: more crucially, they externalize psychological turbulence. They do so by centering around a set of carefully arranged archival materials that the player transforms into a coherent narrative by the way they navigate the given environment.[19] Walking through the home in *What Remains of Edith Finch* yields a dramatic retelling of a family's tragic history, and in *Gone Home*, the protagonist uncovers recent events of her family while searching through an empty parental home, in what Marie-Laure Ryan would call "internal–exploratory interactivity."[20] The mansions and country houses of these two games are typically modern: they recall the settings of novels by Virginia Woolfe, E.M. Forster, and other members of the Bloomsbury Group. These authors drew on critical, progressive, and Freudian insights to explore personal relationships and private lives, often through labyrinthine narrative structures involving shifting perspectives and embedded stories. The mansion offered a perfect backdrop for a cast of

Figure 4.1 Navigation in *Firewatch*. Author screenshot.

diverse characters—servants as well as masters—to come together and fall apart.

Melissa Kagen comments on the regularity with which walking simulators focus on death, allowing the player to bear witness instead of causing death around them.[21] The same is the case for *What Remains of Edith Finch*, in which you play the titular character Edith as she explores her ancestral home with the goal of understanding the history of her allegedly cursed family. Built haphazardly, this surrealist house seems even bigger inside than from the outside. Throughout the course of the game, it becomes a framing device for a range of vignettes about Edith's family members and their tragic deaths, each of which involves new gameplay mechanics.

One such vignette involves Lewis Finch, a young man who works at a cannery. His job is to cut the heads off fish that come down a conveyor belt. As Lewis becomes dissatisfied with his mundane, repetitive life, he begins to retreat into a fantasy world inside his head. The player performs the fish-cutting task with one hand (one side of the controller) while simultaneously navigating Lewis's increasingly elaborate and detailed fantasy world with the other. In spatializing psychological distress, games like *Edith Finch* can be read as a typically modern form of travel writing, involving a symbolic correlation between the interiors of a place and the mind.[22] Players explore the corners of intimate personal relations and subjectivity, often through deliberate, slow movement.

Contrary to the promise of a diversity of areas, biomes, and settings—a common advertising strategy for games that we saw, for instance, in the *Visit Xbox* campaign from Chapter 2—walking sims force the player to stay longer in one place, getting to know the area and the people living in it. In *Edith Finch*, you can pick up a photograph and hold it in front of you, and she will start narrating about her grandfather. You are not just an observer, you are inhabiting her; not just seeing with fresh eyes, but through her eyes. These walking sims show that touristic desire is also a narrative desire to view the world from a different perspective: what it is like to be someone else, to exist somewhere else, if only for a while. It is a different type of escape: one into someone else's experience. Walking through the Finch residence is not based on the promise that *you can go there*, but on the experience of being submersed in someone else's story, of quite literally "living like a local."

This insistence on connecting with local cultures and people, a preoccupation with authenticity instead of spectacle, also hints at a clear marker of cultural capital that connects the walking sim to the current appetite for slow and immersive tourism, a travel philosophy that encourages travelers to engage with local culture rather than trying to see as many attractions as quickly as possible. If slow tourism is opposed to mass tourism—not just passing through but wanting to *soak it up*—walking sims are similarly opposed to mass games: they are not about immersion via power fantasy, but about immersion through empathy; by taking in the details of the story when piecing it together.

Tellingly, the walking sim typically includes elements that are set up against the trappings of modern, digital technology. *Gone Home* and *What Remains of Edith Finch* take place in old family homes with wooden floors, old radio sets, piled-up books, and not a flat-screen TV in sight. The latter game also includes many "analog" haunted house contraptions like trap doors and rotating bookcases. *Firewatch*, set in the 1980s, forces players to navigate the park using the "analog" means of a map and compass. The preoccupation with old-fashioned technology and natural materials, related to what Totten called "homely places," is demonstrative of a genre that forces the player to slow down and feel a sense of nostalgia for simpler times.

My use of directives here is central: walking sims are not about learning new skills or creatively dealing with problems in a different way. They are meant to be played obediently. The influence of the *dérive* returns here, as Debord was careful to point out that this way of walking does not mean ambling about randomly. The effects of geographical locations on people's emotions and behavior are not a matter of chance, he noted, but delineated by "contours, with constant currents, fixed points, and vortexes that strongly discourage entry into or exit from certain zones." Walking simulators encode this idea of "discouraging entry" quite literally: they take place in relatively closed-off spaces and often contain "invisible walls": boundaries that limit where a player can go, but that do not appear as physical obstacles.

The invisible wall has a lot in common with the "keep off grass" and "off-limits" signposts one finds at popular tourist sites. The insistence on a manicured experience, in this sense, has more in common with a mass tourist experience than the subversive nature of slow tourism, typified by individual idiosyncrasies and a desire to go beyond the carefully laid out scripts the tourism industry offers to its customers. In fact, walking sims may complicate the player-character's psychology, or the narrative of the place they wander through, but they rarely focus on the act of walking itself. In this regard, the term "walking sim" is somewhat misleading: walking is presented here as an almost implicit matter that rarely draws attention to itself as an embodied activity.[23]

Instead, the dominant sense activated in the walking sims is one's sight. Tellingly, at one point in *Firewatch,* players find a disposable cardboard camera with most of the film still available. They are then encouraged to take some snaps of interesting scenery. Once players have filled their film, a menu option becomes available that allows them to process the images and deliver them to their physical house as glossy photographs. The attractiveness of procuring such touristic memorabilia shows that distinctions between physical and virtual gazing are increasingly blurred. Perhaps it is more accurate to call these walking sims "gazing sims," building on meaning-making through visual cues. In *Firewatch*, it is specifically a tourist gaze, focused on the landscape instead of the body traversing it.

Going Off Script

At this point, it is worth noting that not all walking sims require the player to stay on a neatly curated path. As game designer David Szymanski has said, the term "walking sim" is a confusing name, with "a lot of different games and philosophies that fall under it."[24] Games such as *Gone Home* and *Firewatch* tend to reduce the space for player action in order to tell a narrative. By piecing together an archive of clues, the player completes the narrative.

One of the genre's earliest examples, *The Path*,[25] is a psychological horror game that offers a variation on the story of "Red Riding Hood." You can choose to control one of six different sisters who are sent one-by-one on errands by their mother to see their sick grandmother. You have to decide whether to follow the "safe" route that has been laid out for you, or to venture off the beaten path and explore the more dangerous, uncharted areas of the forest—including, of course, the Wolf. You *can* go to grandmother's house while staying on the path: you will arrive safely, cozy up next to grandmother, and be sent back to the apartment you came from in a somewhat anticlimactic ending. The game's exploration and horror aspects—what most would call the game itself—are only revealed if you depart from the path. "Going off script," in other words, is a central operation of the script itself.

For a more recent example of this kind of encoded defiance, we can turn to *The Stanley Parable* (*TSP*),[26] a first-person walking simulator originally released as a mod for *Half-life 2* by game designers Davey Wreden and William Pugh. In the game, the player guides a silent protagonist named

Stanley through a 90s-style office space, alongside narration by British actor Kevan Brighting. As you explore the office space, you are confronted with diverging pathways, and are offered all kinds of ways to follow or diverge from the story told by the paternalistic narrator, who becomes the game's primary antagonist. Walking through particular doors or hallways triggers his catechistic commentary, telling you what to do, what you did, what Stanley is or isn't thinking, and what the narrator himself thinks of all of the choices you make. Because the narrator frequently remarks on Stanley's actions before they have been taken, you can rebel against the despotic narrator. Following or escaping their guidance at different points in the office halls, you end up on one of the game's many narrative paths.

TSP is a form of ergodic metafiction that reflects on the limitations of interactive narrative,[27] but it also essentially responds to the problem of touristic freedom in video games, and the pervasiveness of the myth that *you can go there*. It does so in a typical postmodern move that draws attention to the form of the medium. In her book *Metafiction*, literary critic Patricia Waugh discusses self-reflexive postmodern literature as responding to the problem of representation:

> The metafictionist is highly conscious of a basic dilemma: if he or she sets out to "represent" the world, he or she realizes fairly soon that the world, as such, cannot be "represented." In literary fiction it is, in fact, possible only to "represent" the discourses of that world. Yet, if one attempts to analyse a set of linguistic relationships using those same relationships as the instruments of analysis, language soon becomes a "prisonhouse" from which the possibility of escape is remote. Metafiction sets out to explore this dilemma.[28]

To highlight the self-reflexivity of its gameplay, *TSP* plays in an office, and a dreadfully boring one at that, with cubicles and slide decks with satirical tips on "how to solve a dispute with a co-worker" and "using slides to assure employees that everything is okay."

The reflection on freedom here is also a reflection on office culture, what David Graeber called bullshit jobs,[29] and the "freedom" of workers in a society that produces for the market. An office is a place where you follow orders, where you are integrated into a web of meaning that provides purpose to your days, that provides concerns that you can keep thinking about when you drive home, and that in time becomes difficult to imagine your days without. The absurdity of this endeavor is reflected in the narrator's first lines during the game's opening cutscene:

> Stanley worked for a company in a big building where he was employee number 427. Employee number 427's job was simple: he sat at his desk in room 427 and he pushed buttons on a keyboard [...] Stanley relished every

Bigger on the Inside 59

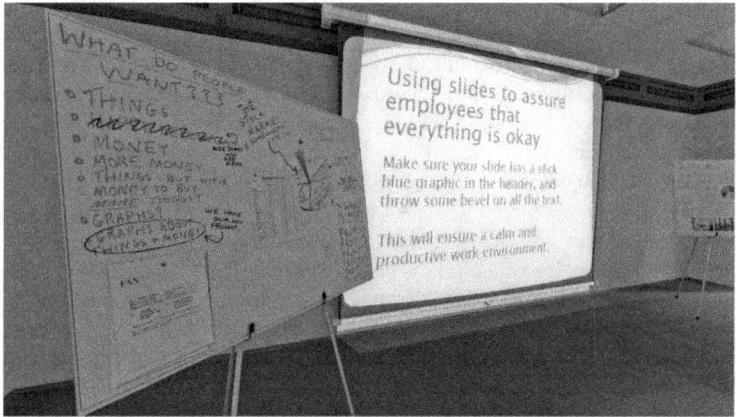

Figure 4.2 Office culture in *The Stanley Parable*. Author screenshot.

moment that the orders came in, as though he had been made exactly for this job. And Stanley was happy.

As the player is given control, the camera pans into Stanley's field of view, facing his computer screen, mirroring how the player is facing theirs. This is one of the several ways in which *TSP* deliberately triggers a confusion between Stanley and the player. Apart from the opening cutscene, not a lot is known about Stanley, and the narrator frequently addresses Stanley as "you" when requesting he performs an action. On several occasions, you are the one pressing the buttons that the narrator recounts as being pressed by Stanley.

It is through this confusion of subjectivity that *TSP* questions the difference between (digital) labor and play. It not only highlights the procedural limitations of video games—questioning if real "choices" even exist within their confines—but it also offers a space to reflect on a more common consumerist dictum of individual autonomy, spurred on not in the last place by algorithmic systems. In the realm of tourism, this ideology of solipsistic liberty is pursued most readily on platforms such as Airbnb or TripAdvisor, which promise their customers the possibility of self-dependency and "travel" (as opposed to tourism) by comparing and contrasting their options in a highly granular way. As I've written elsewhere, the allure of these platforms is that they are constructed as disruptors of the mass tourism industry, allowing individuals to stay in local people's apartments and visit local restaurants and bars, instead of being forced onto the "beaten path" of touristic experience.[30] Of course, in doing so, these platforms create their own forms of digital dependence (if not addiction), as our explosive use of social media shows.

This process is captured in one of *TSP*'s many endings, called the "freedom ending." It involves Stanley obeying *everything* the narrator says in order to, ironically, destroy a "Mind Control Facility" he was allegedly controlled by. After pushing a big "OFF" button, a large hangar door dramatically slides open, and you step out of the building into a green field. The narrator muses: "He had defeated the machine, unshackled himself from someone else's command. Freedom was mere moments away." But as soon as Stanley steps out of the hangar and into the lush vista, a sight reminiscent of so many other games, the player loses control. "This was exactly the way, right now, that things were *meant* to happen," declares the narrator as the screen fades to white. "And Stanley was happy." The observant player remembers this line from the game's opening, in which Stanley was introduced as a brainwashed employee pushing buttons on demand. The question the player is left with is whether they had any meaningful agency in choosing to follow the script, or if their compliance was a matter of blissful ignorance and false consciousness.

Tellingly, after the initial release of *TSP*, the designers created a trailer called "The Stanley Parable: Raphael Trailer." The trailer responds to an angry email they received from a disappointed player calling themselves Raphael. The narrator voices the email in a highly satirical tone: "I felt like I was being taken into someone else's hallways, doors and plans, to deliver me an experience that didn't touch me [...] People play games because of what they can do inside them, and your game is very good at letting them know they can't do anything."[31]

The narrator then notes he rebuilt the game from the ground up, "to capture not just many emotions, but *all* emotions." The trailer proceeds to show a bicycle laying sideways on the concrete, with the promise that players can do "literally anything" with it. The joke highlights the main conceit that *TSP* reflects on: that there can be such a thing as total representation, and that the most devious aspect of systems of control is the sense of *internal* freedom they provide to their subjects. The sense of scope it enables is primarily due to the many different paths and endings the player can explore. It allows them to explore the tensions between compliance and insubordination, and to interrogate the common myth of video games in which, as Lev Manovich put it, "the user is expected to inhabit the mind of the designer and mistake it for their own."[32]

Resignation and Subversion

In *The Stroll as a Storytelling Model*, Claudia Albes makes a distinction between narratives that feature walking or wandering protagonists, versus literature that uses those acts as formal metaphors by leaping around through footnotes or other means.[33] A similar observation can be made about walking sims: some are, indeed, about walking through a mansion or national park. This does not mean, however, that they take an interest in the physicality of walking.

For an example of a game that formalizes walking, we can turn to *Journey*,[34] a third-person game in which you play a nameless robed avatar making its way to a mountain in the distance. *Journey* can be considered a walking sim due to its lack of fail state and focus on exploration, but it deviates from former examples in that it does not take place in one space, and is not so much about piecing together a story as it is about moving through an environment. It is not primarily about discovering a narrative but a "sensation of wandering," as game designer Ed Key calls it.[35] As I have written elsewhere, *Journey* allows players to playfully approximate the locomotive dynamics of pilgrimage—more specifically, the ebb and flow of hardship and prosperity, dejection and euphoria, of which the pilgrim's itinerary consists.[36]

The key procedures in *Journey* are climbing, surfing, jumping, and gliding. The ways in which these forms of locomotion are modeled are key to the experience: the slowing down and laborious bodily gestures of your nameless avatar when trudging uphill are complemented by the effortless feeling of surfing down dunes. Through these mechanics, *Journey* shows how certain pleasures of playing a video game are kinesthetic, a series of "embodied events" in which particular forms of movement relate to particular emotional responses.[37] Acceleration, for instance, is coupled with resignation: this is most clear during surfing sections in which the player-character slides down vast hills of sand, straight toward a mountain, unable to stop. You can slightly swerve left and right, but you have to relinquish control and accept the momentum in which you are captured.

The importance of these locomotive dynamics is most notable in the final act of the game. As you scale the final mountain slope in a snowstorm, battered by the wind, any movement becomes increasingly difficult. After you collapse and seemingly succumb to the weather, the screen fades to white and the music fades away. Then, in a sudden moment of visual and aural animation, you are thrust upwards, and the ensuing final section of the game involves a sequence of ecstatic elevation. Rising above the clouds, in a blissful, paradise-like setting, you can effortlessly fly upward to the final mountaintop.

Journey is a game that asks to be played obediently, as a rite or form of pilgrimage. The trek to the mountain compresses the concept of an epic journey into a 90-minute experience in which it is tempting to follow the game's clever and understated nudges. These include the camera panning towards the mountain at specific moments to remind the player of where they need to go, as well as gusts of wind that prevent the player from straying off the intended path.

However, it is because of its focus on physicality—literally, the physics systems the game employs—that *Journey* allows for particular forms of disobedience and subversive wandering.

Players have found a range of exploits of environmental and control glitches: one resulting technique involves going "out of bounds," by moving through walls or corners at precisely the right spot so as to leave the authorized play area. But *Journey* also allows for physics-driven techniques, assembled in a sanctioned modality of playing called "Expert Mode" by the player community. One of the associated techniques is called "fancy flying," and it involves controlling both the camera and the player-character in order to gather energy with a dive and release it in the form of a boost. As the *Journey Wiki* notes: "A player who is skilled in fancy flying is often called a Fancy Flyer. For a fancy flyer, FF is a whole different gameplay and approach to Journey which delivers lots of fun and fulfillment."[38]

These subversive forms of play draw on a desire to go beyond the authored experience. It is a typically touristic inclination. Sociologist Dean MacCannell, inspired by Erving Goffman's distinction between the dramaturgical front and back regions of everyday life, argued that many tourists long to reach past the staged, service-oriented interactions that are part of the "front region" of tourism. More adventurous tourists instead try to experience "back regions" that usually are closed to outsiders—the kitchen, the backyard, the private party—as these are considered to be more authentic, intimate, or real.

There are striking similarities between MacCannell's tourists looking for back regions, and players looking for cracks in code to go "out of bounds" and explore unauthorized or unfinished environments in games. But crucially, it is the physics system of this walking simulator that gives players the opportunity to engage in this search. As Miguel Sicart notes, play repurposes serious things into the non-serious: it takes a serious stair or a handrail and transforms it into something playful.[39] But this does require a skateboard—some kind of somatic means to rub against the world and cause a sense of friction. One way in which games can unthink touristic structures is by emphasizing the physicality of the virtual body.

Walking in Space Boots

I now want to return to a game that plays with the representation of external, instead of internal, magnitude. In the last chapter, we already saw games shrinking down cities and landscapes for the purpose of play. Here, I want to discuss an example of taking this approach to its logical extreme. My case study is *Outer Wilds*,[40] a first-person adventure game in which you uncover a narrative across different planets in a miniature solar system.

While *Outer Wilds* is not easily classified as a walking sim due to its heavy reliance on flight mechanics, it has a lot in common with the other games of this chapter. You play as an astronaut and archeologist on a mission to discover the story of an alien civilization that once lived there. That story is told on walls full of an ancient hieroglyphic language that can be scanned and translated. The player-character is, again, an archivist who fashions a narrative out of a collection of recorded conversations. However, what sets *Outer Wilds* apart is both its sense of extreme spatial compression and intense physicality as the player-character flies and walks across these planets.

Caught in an initially unexplained time loop, the *Outer Wilds* player has 22 minutes to explore the various planets and moons in their solar system before a stellar explosion destroys everything, and the loop restarts. The game's setting, a solar system with several planets, induces a sense of awe–yet it is also clearly miniaturized, with distances measured in kilometers and spaceships cobbled together with wooden planks. It is this antinomy between the sublime and the homespun that lends the game its aesthetic.

In one of the game's most memorable moments, you figure out how to reach a space station orbiting the sun. You open the safety hatch, it falls away, and the sun roars beneath your feet. In this particular moment, the sun feels like a sublime celestial body, as grand as it is deadly. It is a paradoxical experience, as you can literally see the sun's curvature, and the space you are exploring is evidently modeled, trifling compared to the thing it is standing in for.

The sublime is often connected to the sense of size that many modern exploration games create. Paul Martin, for instance, discusses how *The Elder Scrolls IV: Oblivion* "is encountered in the sublime mode [through] an incomprehensible largeness and expanse."[41] But it is worth remembering David Hume's point that *size* and *scale* are not the same thing. The scale of a thing is the size appropriate to its function; the "scale" for human things is the human body and its capacities. Scales are not expressed in absolute units; they are a comparative relation. You need two scales to talk about scale at all.[42]

The dramatic sense of scale in *Outer Wilds* has to do with the player projecting their own scale of things onto this imaginary one. The sun is enormous, even if it is a model. This game is, essentially, a compilation of these kinds of moments: it includes a tornado-filled ocean and a black hole looming at the center of a crumbling planet. All of these cosmic phenomena are scaled down, while also retaining the qualities needed for a sublime encounter.

Alex Beachum, the Creative Director of *Outer Wilds*, has professed being inspired by the Legend of Zelda series.[43] It is striking that the word "wild" appears both in this game's title and in *BOTW*: it suggests both natural expansiveness, unpredictability and danger, and a sense of exploration. But another parallel is the way in which the world is miniaturized. As I noted in Chapter 1, Shigeru Miyamoto once mentioned how he viewed Zelda as "a miniature garden that you can put into a drawer and revisit anytime you like."[44] *Outer Wilds* takes this design philosophy of the diorama to its logical extreme, placing the player-character into a miniature solar system that explicitly acts as a metonym.

That dualism of scales, I want to argue, is what makes the game stand out among its space simulator contemporaries, as well as the games I have been discussing so far. *Outer Wilds* does attempt to create a perceived sense of

64 *Bigger on the Inside*

Figure 4.3 The toy solar system of *Outer Wilds*. Author screenshot.

accuracy in representing the scale of its phenomena. The player's home planet has maybe two dozen people on it, in one little village consisting of a handful of houses, and villagers who all know each other by name. The Nomai, the race of aliens that the player-character investigates, similarly consists of around thirty individuals. At the same time, they are presented as spacefaring races that have developed appropriate technology. The game never really resolves the tension between these scales. Time is similarly compressed—the solar system dies out in about twenty minutes—but remains uncompressed in other ways. For instance, players learn that the Nomai arrived and died in their solar system hundreds of thousands of years ago, and that time frame significantly adds to the sense of scale and tragedy. *Outer Wilds* acts as a model, but crucially, not all the time.

The game uses a metaphor to bridge this gap between the minute and the humongous: space travel as camping in the woods. There is a quirkiness to the race of aliens the player inhabits: they roast marshmallows in the forest, their scientific ambitions have a do-it-yourself aesthetic of timber and duct tape, and the whole game is accompanied by a quaint banjo-led soundtrack. These moments give the game a distinct warmth, lighting up the coldness of space and the icy synthesizers typically used to represent it.

However, these are only moments. The game's quirky aesthetics clash with its relatively accurate simulation of orbital gravity and space flight. It is notably hard to navigate your spaceship around, and especially at the beginning, players are likely to be bumping against walls, or clumsily flying into objects. Tellingly, and like the Legend of Zelda series, the game features a silent protagonist, meaning it is not so much about exploring the player-character's subjectivity as it is about inhabiting their body. Added to this is the decisive materiality of the game's planets, with shifting sands, falling rocks, and currents dotted throughout the solar system. There are many ways to die in *Outer Wilds*: players can be squashed by rising sand, fly into the sun, get smashed onto the ground—all of it from a first-person perspective, with the HUD of their space suit flickering, and the sound effects of cracking bones or burned skin. The player-character's corporeality is constantly italicized.

Like *Journey*, the physicality of movement is accentuated by the game's physics engine. There is a sense of joy in crashing into the game's toy planets, figuring out how to land safely, and eventually learning how to perform impressive feats like matching the speed of a space station, which the game hands out achievements for. It is this operationalization of the basics of Newtonian gravity that, I would argue, allows *Outer Wilds* to subvert the kinds of alienation that come with gazing alone. It shows that the physical control we have is also the control to subvert, to object, to uncomfortably bump against the world or crash into it headfirst.

It sets up a dynamic of both control and surrender. The time loop in *Outer Wilds* plays a constitutive role in this process: every 22 minutes the player-character gets to witness the end of the universe, as the sun explodes into a supernova that engulfs the solar system. The observant player will also begin to note that the same is happening with all stars in the sky as the loop comes to an end.

The vastness of all the sublime objects and catastrophic events in *Outer Wilds*—planets and stars and the end of the universe itself—came into clear focus after I turned off the console and sat in a room with the controller on my lap, glancing at the night sky through my window. The game complicates the sublime by being so evidently miniaturized, and so clearly handcrafted. The act of play oscillates between being thrown around in the model and overseeing it; between the control of puzzling together a narrative, and the lack of control over ecological catastrophe.

Film scholar Scott Bukatman has pointed out that "the precise function of science fiction, in many ways, is to create the boundless and infinite stuff of the sublime experience."[45] But what makes *Outer Wilds* interesting in the context of games and tourism is that it defamiliarizes players from the common ways in which the sublime is performed. Where *BOTW*, discussed in the previous chapter, complicates the sublime by focusing on the minute as much as on the grandiose, *Outer Wilds* does so by miniaturizing the solar system, which allows the game to present environmental crisis in a startling way. It is hard not to be reminded of the planet we ourselves inhabit, and the lack of control we may feel about the ecological disaster that looms at our own scale.

The games in this chapter are defined by their attention to the intersection of space and psychology. But we also saw them catering to a touristic need to "go beyond" the transient experience; to not just visit but to inhabit a space or body. In the next chapter, I will continue pursuing this thread.

Notes

1. Bozdog and Galloway, "Performing Walking Sims," 23.
2. Kagen, *Wandering Games*, 10.
3. Juul, "Aesthetics," para. 4.
4. Davidson, "Shigeru Miyamoto."
5. Derrida, "Structure, Sign, and Play," 212.
6. Salen and Zimmerman, *Rules of Play*, 378-387.
7. Pinchbeck, "Dear Esther," 187.
8. The Chinese Room, *Dear Esther*.
9. Zimmerman & Huberts, "From Walking Simulator," 31.
10. Totten, *An Architectural Approach*, 112.
11. Totten, *An Architectural Approach*, 291.
12. The Fullbright Company, *Gone Home*.
13. Campo Santo, *Firewatch*.
14. Giant Sparrow, *What Remains of Edith Finch*.
15. Carbo-Mascarell, "Walking Simulators," 8.
16. Solnit, *Wanderlust*, 85-6.
17. Debord, "Theory of the Dérive," para. 1 and 2.
18. Ditum, "Firewatch review," para. 4.
19. Kagen, *Wandering Games*, 48.
20. Ryan, "Beyond Myth and Metaphor."
21. Kagen, *Wandering Games*, 62.
22. Das and Youngs, *The Cambridge History of Travel Writing*, 8.
23. Stark, "Unsettling Embodied Literacy," 49.
24. Kill Screen Staff, "Is it time to stop," para. 11.
25. Tale of Tales, *The Path*.
26. Galactic Café, *The Stanley Parable*.
27. Fest, "Metaproceduralism," 1.
28. Waugh, *Metafiction*, 3-4.
29. Graeber, *Bullshit Jobs*.
30. Van Nuenen, *Scripted Journeys*, 14.
31. stanleyparable, "Raphael Trailer."
32. Manovich, *The Language of New Media*, 61.
33. Albes, *Der Spaziergang als Erzählmodell*. For an example of a wandering novel, see Julio Cortázar's *Hopscotch* (1966).
34. Thatgamecompany, *Journey*.
35. Kill Screen Staff, "Is it time to stop," para. 52.
36. Van Nuenen, *Scripted Journeys*, 466.
37. Newman, "The Myth of the Ergodic Videogame," para. 5.
38. Journey Wiki, "Fancy Flying."
39. Sicart, *Play Matters*, 11.
40. Mobius Digital, *Outer Wilds*.
41. Martin, "The Pastoral and the Sublime."
42. Woods, "Scale Critique for the Anthropocene," 134.
43. Noclip, "The Making of Outer Wilds."
44. Parkin, "The Dazzling Reinvention of Zelda."
45. Bukatman, "The Artificial Infinite," 267.

References

Albes, Claudia. *Der Spaziergang als Erzählmodell: Studien zur Jean-Jacques Rousseau, Adalbert Stifter, Robert Walser und Thomas Bernhard*. Tübingen: Francke, 1999.

Binary Systems. *Starflight*. Electronic Arts. Amiga. 1986.
Borges, Jorge Luis. *A Universal History of Infamy*, translated by Norman Thomas de Giovanni. London: Penguin, 1975.
Bozdog, Mona, and Dayna Galloway. "Performing Walking Sims: From Dear Esther to Inchcolm Project." *Journal of Gaming & Virtual Worlds* 12, no. 1 (2020): 23–47, doi:10.1386/jgvw_00003_1.
Bukatman, Scott. "The Artificial Infinite: On Special Effects and the Sublime." In *Post-War Cinema and Modernity: A Film Reader*, edited by John Orr and Olga Taxidou, 214. New York: New York University Press, 2001.
Burke, Edmund. *On the Sublime and Beautiful*. London: Routledge & Kegan Paul, 1961 [1759].
Campo Santo. *Firewatch*. Campo Santo. PlayStation 4. 2016.
Carbo-Mascarell, Rosa. "Walking Simulators: The Digitisation of an Aesthetic Practice." *Proceedings of 1st International Joint Conference of DiGRA and FDG*. Dundee, Scotland (2016): 1–15.
Das, Nandini, and Tim Youngs. *The Cambridge History of Travel Writing*. Cambridge: Cambridge University Press, 2019.
Davidson, John. "Shigeru Miyamoto on Mario, 'Minecraft' and Working With Apple." *Glixel*, December 12, 2016, https://www.rollingstone.com/culture/culture-news/shigeru-miyamoto-on-mario-minecraft-and-working-with-apple-106277/.
Debord, Guy. "Theory of the Dérive." *Les Lèvres Nues* 9, November 1956.
DeKoven, Bernie. *The Well-Played Game: A Player's Philosophy*. Cambridge: MIT Press, 2013.
Derrida, Jacques. "Structure, Sign, and Play in the Discourse of the Human Sciences." In *Modern Criticism and Theory: A Reader*, edited by David Lodge and Nigel Wood, 210–24. London: Routledge, 2013.
Ditum, N. "Firewatch Review—A Small Game with a Big Story." *The Guardian*, February 8, 2016, https://www.theguardian.com/technology/2016/feb/08/firewatch-review-first-person-simulation-adventure-game.
Fest, Bradley J. "Metaproceduralism: The Stanley Parable and the Legacies of Postmodern Metafiction." *Wide Screen* 6, no. 1 (2016): 1–23.
Galactic Café. *The Stanley Parable*. Galactic Café. Microsoft Windows. 2013.
Giant Sparrow. *What Remains of Edith Finch*. Annapurna Interactive. Microsoft Windows. 2016.
Graeber, David. *Bullshit Jobs: The Rise of Pointless Work, and What We Can Do About it*. New York: Simon & Schuster, 2018.
Hello Games. *No Man's Sky*. Hello Games. PlayStation 4. 2016.
Huizinga, Johan. *Homo Ludens: A Study of the Play-Element in Culture*. New York: Angelico Press, 2016.
Journey Wiki. "Fancy Flying." Accessed June 10, 2023, https://journey.fandom.com/wiki/Fancy_Flying.
Juul, Jesper. "The Aesthetics of the Aesthetics of the Aesthetics of Video Games." *12th International Conference on the Philosophy of Computer Games Conference*. August 13–August 15, Copenhagen, 2018, https://www.jesperjuul.net/text/aesthetics3/.
Kagen, Melissa. *Wandering Games*. Cambridge: MIT Press, 2022.
Kant, Immanuel. *Critique of the Power of Judgment*. Cambridge: Cambridge University Press, 2000.

Kill Screen Staff. "Is it Time to Stop using the Term 'Walking Simulator'?" *Kill Screen*, September 30, 2016, https://killscreen.com/articles/time-stop-using-term-walking-simulator/.

MacCannell, Dean. *The Tourist: A New Theory of the Leisure Class*. New York: Schocken Books, 1976.

Manovich, Lev. *The Language of New Media*. Cambridge: MIT Press, 2001.

Martin, Paul. "The Pastoral and the Sublime in Elder Scrolls IV: Oblivion." *Game Studies* 11, no. 3 (2011), http://gamestudies.org/1103/articles/martin.

Mobius Games. *Outer Wilds*. Annapurna Interactive. Microsoft Windows. 2019.

Newman, James. "The Myth of the Ergodic Videogame." *Game Studies* 2, no. 1 (2002), http://www.gamestudies.org/0102/newman/.

Noclip. "The Making of Outer Wilds—Documentary." YouTube, January 1, 2020, https://www.youtube.com/watch?v=LbY0mBXKKT0.

Nye, David E. *American Technological Sublime*. Cambridge: MIT Press, 1994.

Parkin, Simon. "The Dazzling Reinvention of Zelda." *The New Yorker*, March 8, 2017, https://www.newyorker.com/tech/annals-of-technology/the-dazzling-reinvention-of-zelda.

Pinchbeck, Dan. "Dear Esther: An Interactive Ghost Story Built using the Source Engine." In *Interactive Storytelling. First Joint International Conference on Interactive Digital Storytelling, ICIDS 2008 Erfurt*, edited by Ulrike Spierling and Nicolas Szilas, 51–54. Berlin: Springer, 2008.

Ryan, Marie-Laure. "Beyond Myth and Metaphor—The Case of Narrative in Digital Media." *Game Studies* 1, no. 1 (2001), http://www.gamestudies.org/0101/ryan/.

Salen, Katie, and Eric Zimmerman. *Rules of Play: Game Design Fundamentals*. Cambridge: MIT Press, 2004.

Sicart, Miguel. *Play Matters*. Cambridge: MIT Press, 2014.

Solnit, Rebecca. *Wanderlust: A History of Walking*. London: Penguin, 2001.

stanleyparable. "The Stanley Parable 'Raphael Trailer'." YouTube, July 29, 2012, https://www.youtube.com/watch?v=AZ-IcS7mRSk.

Stark, Doug. "Unsettling Embodied Literacy in QWOP the Walking Simulator." *Journal of Gaming & Virtual Worlds* 12, no. 1 (2020): 49–67.

Tale of Tales. *The Path*. Tale of Tales. Microsoft Windows. 2009.

Thatgamecompany. *Journey*. Sony Computer Entertainment. PlayStation 3. 2012.

The Chinese Room. *Dear Esther*. The Chinese Room. Microsoft Windows. 2012.

The Fullbright Company. *Gone Home*. The Fullbright Company. Microsoft Windows. 2013.

The Late Show with Stephen Colbert. "Sean Murray May Have Replaced Morgan Freeman As God." YouTube, October 3, 2015, https://www.youtube.com/watch?v=ZqeN6hj4dZU.

Totten, Christopher W. *An Architectural Approach to Level Design*. Boca Raton: CRC Press, 2014.

Van Nuenen, Tom. "Procedural (E)motion: Journey as Emerging Pilgrimage." *Journal of Popular Culture* 49, no. 3 (2016), doi:10.1111/jpcu.12417.

Van Nuenen, Tom. *Scripted Journeys*. Berlin: De Gruyter, 2021.

Waugh, Patricia. *Metafiction: The Theory and Practice of Self-Conscious Fiction*. New York: Methuen, 1984.

Woods, Derek. "Scale Critique for the Anthropocene." *The Minnesota Review* 83 (2014): 133–42.
Zimmerman, Felix, and Christian Huberts. "From Walking Simulator to Ambience Action Game: A Philosophical Approach to a Misunderstood Genre." *Press Start* 2, no. 2 (2019): 29–50.

5 You Can Stay Here

In the previous chapters, I've been discussing action-adventure games that treat their players as a particular kind of tourist, and that accommodate a "way of seeing" the world oriented around a sense of domination and control. I also looked at walking simulators, which favor a kind of tourist gaze that turns inward rather than outward. The overarching concern has been with the promise of freedom and self-determination that is central to the myth that *you can go there*. In this chapter, I want to explore types of video games—life sims and survival games—that do not primarily view the player as a passer-by, but as someone who can spend a significant portion of their time within one algorithmic ecology. I will also look at the different ways in which these ecologies are created: both through human creativity and procedural generation.

I want to situate these game genres in the context of digital nomadism and other forms of remote work. I will argue that the increasing focus of the tourism industry on less momentary but still highly spurious forms of travel fits perfectly with the explosive popularity of video game genres that do not revolve around the pioneering spirit of *you can go there*, but rather a common hospitality phrase: *you can stay here*. I view these types of games as a form of "digital nomadism" in their own right—oriented around a highly fluid coming and going, and all about *chores*.

In the *survival* game genre, players are challenged to survive in a hostile, intense, open-world environment, starting with minimal equipment. In order to stay alive, players must craft tools to gather resources and sustenance, create weapons to fend off enemies, and build shelters to sleep in. Survival games often feature randomly or procedurally generated persistent environments and are increasingly playable online, allowing multiple players to interact in a shared world.

Because of their status as "homes," survival games often incorporate some form of procedural generation: automating the creation of data algorithmically, according to guidelines set by the programmer. Not only does this allow for game worlds that are vast in scope, but it also enables a continuous variability that keeps players guessing about what challenges they will face next. My first example of this phenomenon is the survival game *No Man's Sky*.[1]

Scale Matters

No Man's Sky (*NMS*) is a survival game allowing you to traverse a procedurally generated, open-world universe of no less than 18 quintillion planets. Focusing on exploration, you can scavenge for resources, fly around the universe in your spaceship, build bases, engage in dogfights, build colonies, and more. Pitching the game as "a universe-size sandbox," lead developer Sean Murray garnered significant anticipation and hype around the game while showing previews at video games conferences in the early 2010s.[2] On one occasion, he appeared on *The Late Show with Stephen Colbert* in a segment titled "Sean Murray May Have Replaced Morgan Freeman As God."[3]

The interview, introducing the game to a larger American audience, was instructive in terms of the gameplay mechanics it highlighted. The clearest one was that of colonialism and conquest. The Colbert producers peppered Murray's pre-recorded gameplay footage with a running joke: every time Murray would name something, they slapped a custom badge with Colbert's face on it accompanied by a sound effect saying "MINE!" It was a well-played joke, but the idea underneath it did signal the familiar urge for territorial conquest and naming things that so many video games internalize as their main mechanics.

This sense of domination and control stood in stark contrast to the sense of personal insignificance that Murray and his team were trying to evoke in players. You can name planets, sure, but in a universe of 18 quintillion of them, how much does that still mean? In the interview, Murray mentioned they were building an "entire universe," to which Colbert replied incredulously: "By 'entire universe' do you mean something the size of *the universe*?"

Murray's answer to this question, and to similar ones asked by other journalists, caused immense hype for *NMS*. His team had created something that exceeded even their own imagination. At one of the game's demonstrations at E3 in 2015, Murray zoomed out the camera to demonstrate the size of his procedurally generated universe to an audibly excited audience. With a dramatic flair, he pondered: "Now most of these planets have never been visited. Many of them never will be."[4]

In Chapter 2, I argued how the phantasm of complete representation haunts visual media, discussing André Bazin's myth of Total Cinema.[5] *NMS* follows this tradition. What stands out about Murray's presentation is his excitement while zooming out toward algorithmic infinity. The appeal of his monologue can be largely explained by the concept of the sublime that I have been tracing in the previous chapter: the sense of awe and greatness that is often associated with experiences that are vast, powerful, and overwhelming. Most games I have been discussing fill the player with a similar sense of awe—such as the opening screen of *Breath of the Wild* discussed in Chapter 3, or the solar system in *Outer Wilds* from Chapter 4.

72 You Can Stay Here

In Murray's presentation, a particular form of the sublime comes to mind: the mathematical kind. The philosopher Immanuel Kant wrote that the mathematical sublime is not so much about the grandeur of nature, but about the human power of reason. When we look at the starry sky, we are unable to visually grasp the immensity or the infinite nature of the universe (see Figure 5.1). Yet we can marvel at our own cognitive capacity to conceive of infinity. Kant writes how "for the mathematical estimation of magnitude there is, of course, no greatest possible (for the power of numbers extends to infinity)."[6]

This focus on the human power of reason is the bedrock for what later would be called the "technological sublime," which refers to the awe one experiences when confronted with exceptionally advanced or complex technological feats.[7] Modern people still conceive of the cosmos as dauntingly vast, but now we do so because we view it through a framework of mathematics, computer science, genetics, and quantum mechanics—a formidable quantitative ensemble of permutation and probability. *NMS* became an object of popular fascination because it *algorithmically* conceived of 18 quintillion planets; a scale that our imagination could not keep up with. It reminded us that human designers may never be able to bring an actual stand-in for the universe into existence, but our algorithms might just be powerful enough to do so.

When *NMS* was finally released, the game failed to include all the features that Murray had talked about, such as the ability to encounter other players. Beyond that, the team's algorithmic universe was notably monotonous and lifeless. Murray became the target of a harassment campaign organized by hardcore fans, explaining to *The Guardian* how, in the months after the

Figure 5.1 Flying towards a procedurally generated planet in *No Man's Sky*. Author screenshot.

game's release, his company was in regular contact with Scotland Yard and the Metropolitan police.

The cause of this toxicity was not so much an issue of size, but one of detail. The promise of an infinite map also causes hyperbolic imagination about its minutia. In the interview, Murray notes the absurdity of some of these expectations. "I remember getting a death threat about the fact that there were butterflies in our original trailer, and you could see them as you walked past them, but there weren't any butterflies in the launch game."[8]

In the years since, Murray and his team have been adding free downloadable content to *NMS*, leading to a full-blown redemption arc among fans of the game. There is no doubt that all of this labor caused immense strain among the developers, and it demonstrates the cost of disappointment in a medium rife with fan toxicity. *NMS* shows how the promise that *you can go there* can lead to a sense of entitlement that is a shared characteristic of certain players and tourists. I would argue that the toxicity pointed at the game's creators was at least in part aggregated due to the territorial promise of ownership and conquest that this game made.

What makes *NMS* interesting in the context of hospitality is that, despite its size, it is still one big ecology; one universe to exist in, consisting of relatively predictable algorithmic elements. This is where the game's survival elements become relevant. Players must manage their character's survival by attending to their needs for oxygen, food, and water, while also protecting themselves from environmental hazards and hostile creatures. They can gather resources and craft items to meet their survival needs, such as building a base to protect themselves from the elements, repairing their spacecraft, and crafting equipment like exosuits that allow them to explore hazardous environments. Players can also craft weapons to defend themselves against the hostile creatures they may encounter while exploring the game's procedurally generated universe.

NMS repeats a familiar preoccupation with *size*. But at this point, I want to highlight once more that players can be defamiliarized from these preconceptions. As a counterexample to *NMS,* we can look at Obsidian Entertainment's *Grounded*,[9] a whimsical survival game where you have been shrunk to about the size of an ant and dropped in the backyard. The game borrows from the snug aesthetic of 90s movies like *Honey I Shrunk the Kids*, telling a story of four teenagers trapped in a science experiment gone wrong. Trapped in the garden, the player-character must gather resources, craft tools, and weapons, and build shelter in order to survive and uncover the mystery of their shrinking.

Grounded makes it worth pointing out again that size and scale refer to different things. The scale of a thing is the size appropriate to its function; "scale" for human things is the human body and its capacities. Where *NMS* is oriented around a universal size, *Grounded* rescales the garden—one of the most quotidian spaces of most people's lives—as a titanic ecology. *Grounded* puts an ironic spin on Todd Howard's quote about mountains in the distance: "See that molehill? You can go there."

Stray pots and juice boxes become monumental obstacles, while ants and spiders become towering beasts. The player learns to recognize minute aspects of the garden that are overlooked on a human scale, like rolled-up leaves that can be used as tunnels. At one point, the player-character explores the sprawling labyrinth of an anthill. When they reach the other end, they emerge into the garden's sandbox—now an arid desert. The reimagining of these kinds of familiar biomes allows players to recognize the bias towards the human scale that most games share.

To enhance this experience of the grand mundane, *Grounded* cleverly uses a technique of gazing that is not so much human as it is machinic. The game uses an extreme form of "focus pulling"—shifting focus between objects—when the player looks at things that are close or distant. The giant oak tree or the house towering over the garden remains indistinguishably blurry unless you choose to focus on them through the weeds, or from the top of a flower. These kinds of camera techniques produce a response that will be familiar to anyone who has operated a macro-lens in the garden, where objects are suddenly revealed in their detail when the dial is adjusted. But here, it also creates a dichotomy between the minute and the grand, between the common miniature objects the player becomes familiar with and the completely defamiliarized human-scale structures. The shift in focus produces moments of surprise where the player will suddenly recognize that the towering structure they saw in the distance is a forgotten shovel or a garden hose (see Figure 5.2).

Figure 5.2 The gargantuan garden of *Grounded.* Author screenshot.

Through these methods, *Grounded* yields a creative variation on Michael Chabon's novel *The Amazing Adventures of Kavalier and Clay*. In it, the author describes the moment of recognition when one develops a sense of direction in a place.

> He looked up and down the street. He was struck by a sudden sense of connectedness to it, of knowing where it led to. The map of the island—which looked to him like a man whose head was the Bronx, raising an arm in greeting—was vivid in his mind, flayed like an anatomical model to reveal its circulatory system of streets and avenues, of train, trolley, and bus routes.[10]

Chabon's description of New York reveals how the player in *Grounded* is involved in the process of becoming acquainted with an area, a realization of spatial connectedness between streets and pathways. The difference, of course, is that *Grounded* does it for a space one normally steps across in seconds. As we have seen in the last chapter with *Outer Wilds*, what allows video games to defamiliarize players from their touristic imagination is their potential to make creative use of scale. *Outer Wilds* scales down the universe to remind players how vast the real thing is; *Grounded* scales up the garden to show the intricacies and details we normally glance right over, and to reimagine it as a fundamentally inhospitable space. Both games utilize the tension between our imaginative sense of scale and its mediated representation. They both draw on the sublime in order to create a sense of peril and apprehension.

Relaxing Survival

The sandbox games I discussed in Chapter 3 envision spaces that allow for a disinterested, aesthetic gaze—most tellingly, by offering overviews of the sublime landscape or city. They are like tourist brochures that extract all sense of danger from the vista, but at the same time pit the player against all manner of enemies and obstacles. It results in a sense of frontier exploration where momentary conflicts are embedded in the tourist gaze; a necessary condition for the opportunity to explore beautiful environments. Survival games, as I noted, create a more permanent sense of peril.

Survival games stand in the context of novels like *Robinson Crusoe*, movies like *The Hunger Games*, and reality TV shows like *Survivor* and *Naked and Afraid*. They take place in different kinds of inhospitable areas and extreme conditions (the remote island and jungle are staples) which the player has to learn to endure—or better yet, thrive in. This gamification of survival is perfect for the medium of games, and survival games are among the most popular. Examples like *Rust*,[11] *ARK*,[12] and of course, *Minecraft*,[13] can be found high in the "most popular" charts of gaming platforms like Steam.

Survival games are commonly built on the idea of landscape-environment. This is evident in games like *Rust* that play out in typical wilderness settings—but also in *No Man's Sky*, where space is overwhelming, and the hazard lies in the fact we cannot oversee its algorithmic variability. *Grounded* transforms the garden, an environment we typically consider one of the safest spaces in our lives, into a space that is out to kill us.

The popularity of landscapes as a space for survival, and the conceptualization of survival as a leisurely activity, connects games and tourism. This is particularly evident in different forms of adventure and extreme tourism, which are the fastest-growing tourism sectors.[14] They involve travel to perilous places—mountains, jungles, deserts, caves, canyons, and so on—or participation in dangerous events. An adventure tourist going to Peru would rather go camping with Amazonian village locals than take an airconditioned bus to Machu Picchu.

The popularity of these genres of travel and consumption signals a desire for authenticity and sustainability that can be difficult to find in mainstream tourism, which is oriented around comfort. There is a need for a sense of perseverance, endurance, and ingenuity in the face of cruelty. This need is also hard to separate from the societal conditions individuals are raised in. Adventure tourism and survival shows are both responses to, and caused by, the intensification and competitiveness of post-Reagan neoliberalism, where individuals are constantly contending with one another for resources and opportunities. Many cultural critics have commented on the "always-on," urban, digitized lives of the middle class. They are filled with hi-octane careers that take up much more than eight hours per day, and that are deeply connected to people's sense of identity. Survival-as-leisure allows people to replicate this same sense of competition in an encapsulated, ludic setting, with clear winners and losers, and with a clear beginning and end.

Adventure tourism and survival genres also occur at the intersection of technology and the need for a connection with nature. This is paradoxical, as the rise of these genres is no doubt fueled by technology. Adventure tourism is marked by the high-tech gear of the climber, the ease of acquiring information and skills on YouTube, and bragging rights on social media. Video games are a perfect encapsulation of this double bind to both technology and nature: camping in the woods, cutting logs, and hunting wildlife have become some of the most popular gameplay mechanics in modern gaming. It is easy to be skeptical about the potential of a digital medium to bring anyone closer to nature. But I would argue that, clearer than when watching TV shows, games show that the survival genre is always about more than just survival: it's about flourishing, and about building a home.

The best example to mention here is no doubt the sandbox-survival game *Minecraft*, one of the best-selling video games of all time, with over 238 million copies sold in 2021. In *Minecraft*, you explore a procedurally generated world of blocks that is, again, virtually infinite. *Minecraft* originally included 30 types of blocks, but has over the years expanded to include over 150, from cobblestone and sand to gold ore. By placing these blocks in different orders on a three-by-three grid, you can craft an increasingly complex variety of tools, items, and structures. However, the game tells you notably little about what you *can* build. Playing *Minecraft* has over the years become a collectively sourced form of literacy, with millions of "how to" videos detailing the wild variety of things players can do. The game's $2.5 billion US acquisition by Microsoft in 2014 is a testament to its status as a persistent virtual ecology for creativity and pedagogy in which people spend a significant part of their lives.

The original version of *Minecraft* famously includes two modes: Survival and Creative. The latter allows players to build their own world with few restrictions. The relatively short-lived metaverse fantasies touted by social media platforms are no doubt predicated on games like *Minecraft*, where people have created anything from a complete replica of Zelda's Hyrule[15] to a working computer using redstone blocks whose functioning closely reflects binary logic.[16] One can scroll through thousands of YouTube videos revealing *Minecraft* creations of this kind. This lands us once again in the role of the technological sublime: here, however, the incredulity comes from the knowledge that all of these creations were dreamt up by determined human players working within the affordances of the game. You find yourself thinking, "Wait, they *built* this?"

Minecraft is not only about building, however; it is also about surviving *within* what you built. As games scholar Sean C. Duncan has noted, it is the tension between construction and survival that has led to *Minecraft*'s enduring popularity. Players must build protective structures against the monsters that roam around at night, including skeletons, zombies, and the infamous "Creeper." Due to the presence of monsters at night, players are encouraged to dig, uncover new materials, and craft increasingly complex objects while waiting for the sun to rise.[17] The game's creator, Markus Persson, only built in the Survival mode after testing out the Creative mode, which on its own lacked a sense of purpose. The survival mode imbues player construction activities with a sense of consequence: dying to a monster means losing your items, so there is a payoff to building structures and armor.

The home bases players create in *No Man's Sky*, *Grounded*, and most of all *Minecraft* can become beautiful, elaborate, multi-story edifices that they spend months or years chipping away at. It shows how the challenge of the survival genre is not only to navigate the wilderness but to create a proper home in it. What makes these spaces worth staying in is not just the pressure of having to improvise and scavenge in order to stay alive. All the games I have been discussing are also notably calming. You can cut up some wood, build a makeshift shelter, get a fire going, and so on. The auditory experience of these games plays a large role: for an entire generation of players, the music of *Minecraft* has become synonymous with its soothing, gentle qualities.

The paradoxical combination of calmness and anxiety is what makes survival games so alluring, and what explains their enduring popularity. The main mechanic I want to discuss in the remainder of this chapter is that of chores—the small and repetitive tasks that come with living in these persistent worlds, and that show how the mundane is a necessary component of a sense of belonging.

Beyond the clear creative efforts they enable, survival games like *Minecraft* are perhaps best described by their repetitive activities. Playing these games is tantamount to taking on a routine set of chores: everyday but necessary tasks, often in a household setting, that simply need to get done. In *Minecraft*, you manage health and hunger bars by trading bread in villages or killing roaming chickens. *Grounded* employs similar hunger and thirst gauges, asking you to seek out dew drops hanging from grass in the morning, hunt for small insects to roast on a campfire, and so on.

The initial process of getting settled in each of these worlds involves a set of preliminary tasks. For instance, in *Minecraft*, you are first required to build a crafting table. In order to do so, you need to fell a tree to gather some woodblocks. These need to be crafted into wooden planks, which in turn can be transformed into a Crafting Table. With this, you can build other tools such as a pickaxe or shovel, which are needed for tasks such as mining and farming. Then there is the chore of upkeep: survival games offer an array of opportunities to expand and decorate your base with different materials, to construct household appliances, or to put trophies on the wall. After leveling up, your base can be augmented with stronger materials, staircases, and zip lines. Most of these modifications are not required for survival, but encourages you to take up longer-term residence.

It is through these mundane activities that the game world transforms from a touristic destination to something more permanent—and arguably, less continuously oppressive than the word "survival" may suggest. The focus on chores and homemaking connects survival games to a different genre: that of life simulators.

Life's a Chore

Life simulators use the tourist's need to escape from the pace of modern life as their main selling point. *Stardew Valley*,[18] a farming simulator, opens with the player-character—trapped in a tiny gray cubicle—opening a letter from their late grandfather which contains the deed to his farm, purchased at a time in his life when he found himself longing for "real connections with other people and with nature." Following in their grandpa's footsteps, the player-character drops everything and moves to the farm in search of purpose and belonging.

Soon, you find yourself consumed with the daily tasks of farm life: planting, harvesting, and selling crops with hopes of earning enough in-game money to upgrade your farming tools and maybe even purchase some barnyard animals.

Animal Crossing, another popular video game series in the life simulator genre, echoes this ethos. In the series, which was first released in 2001, players take on the role of a human character who moves to a vacation destination and is tasked with building a life for themselves among a cast of anthropomorphic animals. The series' latest entry, *Animal Crossing: New Horizons* (*ACNH*),[19] was released amid global stay-at-home orders during the coronavirus pandemic.

When you begin the game, a Hawaiian-shirt clad raccoon named Tom Nook offers you the opportunity to purchase a "deserted island getaway package." Like *Stardew Valley,* the resonant promise of *ACNH* is not just one of inhabiting a new place, but of making oneself at home and embracing a new way of living. Island living offers the dream of a simpler way of life: the objective of the game is to build a community, make friends with the animal villagers, and create a comfortable and unique living space. You can buy, design, and customize your own homes and visit the homes of other players. You can also interact with the environment by catching fish, collecting insects, completing tasks for the animal villagers, and terraforming the island itself.

One of the defining features of Animal Crossing is its laid-back atmosphere and emphasis on building relationships with the in-game characters. The series follows a real-time clock and calendar, meaning a minute in the game is a minute in the player's clock time. This symmetry gives it a distinct sense of a "parallel universe" that the player can check in with at different points in the day. There are a limited number of small tasks to be done each day, after which you can physically go to sleep before new tasks need to be done.

Players can opt for different levels of involvement, but the completion of everyday tasks is also contextualized by overarching goals. You can donate the fish and insects you catch to a museum. For players aiming to complete all of the game's objectives, there are incentives to log in regularly each day. For example, in *ACNH*, NPCs show up sporadically throughout the course of a two-week time period, some offering various goods for sale and others providing opportunities to sell island wares at a higher price point. If you miss your opportunity to interact with and collect from the NPC of the day, it might be another two weeks before you have the chance to see them again.

Crucially, Animal Crossing plays off of the dream of the white picket fence, offering a gentle take on the debt of home ownership. Most entries in the series begin with the player-character having taken out a loan from Tom Nook to pay for their house. Throughout the course of the game, you must pay off this debt to Tom Nook by earning Bells, the in-game currency. This can be done by selling items they collect, completing tasks for the animal villagers, and participating in various activities in the game world. Paying off the debt is an important aspect of the game, as it allows you to upgrade your house and purchase new items for the island. The burden of debt is significantly reduced, however, as you can work to pay it off at your own pace. What remains of it is something that needs to get done for a sense of accomplishment instead of necessity.

It is this sense of accomplishment of day-to-day activity and chores without the real-world consequences that define the Animal Crossing series—whether it's chopping wood, building a bridge, or gardening, the gameplay loop is about seeing small improvements every day. Game designer Jennifer Scheurle refers to this concept of soothing labor as "gentle progression,"[20] while game scholar Ian Bogost has noted that Animal Crossing "simulates the social dynamics of a small town but sidesteps the material obsession of keeping up with the Joneses."[21] It is entrepreneurial—paying off loans and growing a sales business—but it is also about meandering in a small town (see Figure 5.3).

These dynamics of meandering and casual entrepreneurship are further consolidated by the game's social aspects. Animal Crossing has often been referred to as a "social simulation" series due to its ability to create a sense of community among its human players. *ACNH*, for instance, allows you to invite other player-characters onto your island to show them around, exchange items, and so on. Several studies have explored how the game satisfied key psychological needs of people in lockdown, such as autonomy, relatedness, and competence.[22] But the series' enduring popularity also needs to be connected to broader cultural tensions around career-oriented lives, corporate culture, and managing "work-life balance."

Figure 5.3 Meandering in *Animal Crossing: New Horizons*. Author screenshot.

There is a common sense of shame around time-consuming games, whether the Animal Crossing series or *Minecraft*. Putting a lot of time into video games is considered "wasting time." But what we sometimes derisively call chores is also just work that is less demanding, in that it does not take all day, and does not have to be an integral part of your identity.

Labor journalist Sarah Jaffe has pointed out that the myth around many low-paying careers is that they ought to emerge, primarily, out of passion.[23] This neoliberal ideology of the "labor of love" has been long used to justify the exploitation of workers and to discourage collective action among them. Employers, keen to exploit human capital to its fullest potential, use various strategies to encourage or demand that employees adopt work-centered identities and lifestyles.[24] This is particularly relevant for people in the creative class—which includes conventional knowledge workers as well as people in arts, design, media, science, engineering, education, computer programming, and research. The expectation that these workers should be emotionally invested in their jobs is often used as a justification for low pay and long hours.[25] The effects of overwork, burnout, and a lack of work-life balance are well-known. The promise is that one can appropriate the world through one's activities and products; the Marxian reality is one of increased alienation towards one's labor and the world.[26]

Urban studies theorist Richard Florida situates this phenomenon in the metropolitan city. He notes that cities are more successful and competitive in the global economy when a larger share of their workforce is made up of members of the creative class, and as such are embroiled in an arms race for jobs and talent. Florida argues that these people cluster in cosmopolitan centers due to productivity advantages, economies of scale, and knowledge spillover, encouraging people to work more intensely than they would otherwise. The cyclical result is one of "higher rates of innovation, greater economic prosperity, higher living standards, and more stimulation."[27] The "always-on" mentality that accompanies these careers has only been intensified in recent years, with business collaboration platforms such as Zoom or Slack leading to increased corporate surveillance and (self-)monitoring.

The opposite of "wasted time," so readily connected to video game play, is time that is spent towards personal fulfillment. Western creative class individuals engage in careers that take up much of their lives with the promise of such gratification. Jaffe's point is that our jobs increasingly demand not just our time, but our very existence. Then take a game like *ACNH*: you can engage in work, and then drop it when you feel like it. You can be as demanding of yourself as you want. The immense popularity of these games, I would argue, is for a large part explained by the alternative image of work they foster.

This not only goes for Animal Crossing. I am also thinking here of casual management games such as *Homescapes*[28] and *Farmville*,[29] in which players manage or restore a house, farm, garden, or company. There is a wide variety of such casual games on mobile devices, offering little chores to be performed during the peripatetic, commuting parts of people's days. It may seem remarkable that individuals who spend most of their lives embroiled in work devote their free time to more work, but it is the kind of manageable tasks and evident sense of progression that distinguishes them from the milestone markers of a typical career.

This is not to say that careers are in need of more gamification, as authors such as Jane McGonical have insisted.[30] It is to say that these games are popular because they yield another attitude towards work by offering a type of it that is deescalated, lower-stakes, and less intense. Animal Crossing offers a comfortable monotony allowing players to unwind. The predictability of chores connects life sims and casual games to the survival genre exemplified by *Minecraft* and *Grounded*. What we call "survival" in games is, in fact, mostly about chores, about rather mundane activity instead of a Darwinian "survival of the fittest." Having to scavenge for food every day is not spectacular. This is what makes it appealing. It is through daily, low-stakes activities that we can attain a relationship with a place that is *homely*.

At this point, it also becomes clear that the appeal of these games is fundamentally different from the games I have been discussing so far. They are not grounded in an aesthetic and ideology of tourism, insofar as a lot of tourism under neoliberal tenets is about the intensification of production and consumption. As I pointed out in Chapter 3, tourism is all too readily turned into a relentless checking off of boxes, a successive appropriation of spectacular sights. This is also the reason why so many people come back from a trip more exhausted than they were before they left.

There is another popular form of travel that better explains the popularity of life sims and survival games. I am thinking of digital nomadism and other remote work structures and lifestyles that have rapidly gained popularity in the past decade, and even more so since the coronavirus pandemic. Digital nomadism has exploded in a dual context of urbanism and digitalization. The peer-to-peer accommodation platform Airbnb and its slogan "belong anywhere"[31] are a useful example. Airbnb has been at the forefront of shifting modalities of travel, with many of its hosts offering discounted long-term rental options for people engaged in remote work.

Through changing touristic infrastructures spearheaded by companies such as Airbnb, the creative classes of the Global North are increasingly able to treat other countries and cities as a "home away from home." A recent study by freelancing platform Upwork anticipated that around 40.7 million American professionals will be fully remote in the next five years alone.[32] As sociologists Woldoff and Litchfield have written, digital nomads live lives that are episodic, transitory, and compartmentalized, in nomadic communities with "simultaneously high levels of fluidity and intimacy."[33] The authors' ethnographic study of digital nomads in Bali highlights how the digital nomad lifestyle is an attempt to recover a life that was previously characterized by "all work, no play": being stressed, overworked, deprived of free time, and having difficulty maintaining healthy living, meaningful relationships, and creative endeavors.

At the same time, the digital nomads' low-stakes, disaffected relation to place brings to mind the figure of the flâneur, previously discussed in Chapter 3. As a symbol for people's relationships in modernity, the flâneur is the personification of a cultural change: "from the patient engagement with some object or structure of meaning to a restless wandering, a distracted perceptive style and way of life."[34]

My point is that games like *Minecraft* and the Animal Crossing series offer a virtual engagement that is not all that different from what digital nomads in places like Bali, Medellín, or Cape Town are chasing: a sense of simultaneous creativity and escapism; building on something while rejecting "growing roots." It is a lifestyle that allows for transient forms of community and a general tempering of the work attitudes that come with the neoliberal success paradigm. Digital nomadism, like the games I have been discussing, is a form of de-escalation related to socioeconomic and demographic developments in the labor force, which are occurring the world over.[35]

In the West, we have given names to social phenomena such as "quiet quitting," referring to low employee engagement, and to "the Great Resignation," which especially during the coronavirus pandemic saw employees resigning for reasons such as burnout, the desire for greater flexibility, better work-life balance, or better compensation and benefits. The Chinese concepts of 996 work culture (working from 9 to 9, 6 days a week) and the concomitant rise in interest for "light labor" jobs at companies like grocery stores or fast-food restaurants.[36]

I believe the games I have been discussing need to be situated in the same context. Yet it is also necessary to see the paradox at play here: while these games constitute a form of calming digital nomadism, they also dramatically increase people's time in a virtual space, demanding continuous attention and care. They are an alternative to the corporate envisioning of the metaverse—that persistent virtual space where people can have the same work meetings they would at the office. The billion-dollar investments that Meta, Google, Apple, and Amazon have poured into their metaverse division are geared towards the kind of purpose that runs opposite to why people are engaging so intensely with virtual worlds. Series like Animal Crossing are popular precisely because they are, at their core, about a type of work that is less demanding, and less-all-encompassing.

Notes

1 Hello Games, *No Man's Sky*.
2 E.g. Murray, *No Man's Sky, 2014*.
3 The Late Show with Stephen Colbert, "Sean Murray."
4 Murray, *No Man's Sky Gameplay Trailer 2015*.

5 Bazin, *What is Cinema?*
6 Kant, *The Critique of Judgement*, SS25.
7 Nye, *American Technological Sublime*, xv.
8 MacDonald, "No Man's Sky Developer Sean Murray," para. 6.
9 Obsidian, *Grounded.*
10 Chabon, *The Amazing Adventures of Kavalier & Clay*, 166.
11 Facepunch Studios, *Rust.*
12 Studio Wildcard, *Ark: Survival Evolved.*
13 Mojang. *Minecraft.*
14 Janowski et al., "Dimensions of Adventure Tourism," 1.
15 See for instance Grazzy, "I'm Building ALL OF Breath of the Wild in Minecraft."
16 See for instance legomasta99, "Minecraft Computer Engineering."
17 Duncan, "Minecraft, Beyond Construction and Survival," 7.
18 ConcernedApe, *Stardew Valley.*
19 E.g. Nintendo EPD, *Animal Crossing: New Horizons.*
20 Khan, "Why Animal Crossing Is the Game," para. 15.
21 Bogost, *Persuasive Games*, 269.
22 Yee and Sng, "Animal Crossing and COVID-19," 2022.
23 Jaffe, *Work Won't Love You Back.*
24 Reid, "Embracing, Passing, Revealing," 997.
25 Woldoff and Litchfield, *Digital Nomads*, 41.
26 Jaeggi, *Alienation*, 72.
27 Florida, *Who's Your City?*, 30.
28 Playrix, *Homescapes.*
29 Zynga, *Farmville.*
30 McGonical, *Reality is Broken.*
31 See for instance Chesky, "Belong Anywhere."
32 Ozimek, "Future Workforce Report 2021."
33 Woldoff and Litchfield, *Digital Nomads*, 21.
34 Van Leeuwen, "If we are Flâneurs," 301.
35 Hirsch, "The Great Discontent," para. 3.
36 Wang and Wang, "In China, Young People Ditch Prestige Jobs."

References

Bazin, Andre. *What is Cinema? Volume 1.* Berkeley: University of California Press, 1967.
Bogost, Ian. *Persuasive Games: The Expressive Power of Videogames.* Cambridge: MIT Press, 2010.
Böhme, Gernot. *The Aesthetics of Atmospheres*, edited by Jean-Paul Thibaud. London: Routledge, 2017.
Chabon, Michael. *The Amazing Adventures of Kavalier & Clay.* New York: Random House, 2000.
Chesky, Brian. "Belong Anywhere." *Medium*, July 16, 2014, https://medium.com/@bchesky/belong-anywhere-ccf42702d010.
ConcernedApe. *Stardew Valley.* ConcernedApe. Microsoft Windows. 2016.
Duncan, Sean C. "Minecraft, Beyond Construction and Survival." *Well Played* 1 (2011), doi:10.1184/R1/10029221.v1.
Facepunch Studios. *Rust.* Facepunch Studios. Microsoft Windows. 2018.
Florida, Richard. *Who's Your City? How the Creative Economy Is Making Where to Live the Most Important Decision of Your Life.* New York: Basic Books, 2008.

Golumbia, David. "Games Without Play." *New Literary History* 40, no. 1 (2009): 179–204, doi:10.1353/nlh.0.0077.

Grazzy. "I'm Building ALL OF Breath of the Wild in Minecraft (#1)." YouTube, March 17, 2022, https://www.youtube.com/watch?v=DAkIPaaYrMg.

Headlee, Celeste. *Do Nothing: How to Break Away from Overworking, Overdoing, and Underliving.* New York: Harmony, 2020.

Hello Games. *No Man's Sky.* Hello Games. PlayStation 4. 2016.

Hirsch, Peter Buell. "The Great Discontent." *Journal of Business Strategy* 42, no. 6 (2021): 439–42, doi:10.1108/JBS-08-2021-0141.

Jaeggi, Rahel. *Alienation.* New York: Columbia University Press, 2014.

Jaffe, Sarah. *Work Won't Love You Back: How Devotion To Our Jobs Keeps Us Exploited, Exhausted, and Alone.* New York: Bold Type Books, 2021.

Janowski, Ingo, Sarah Gardiner, and Anna Kwek. "Dimensions of Adventure Tourism." *Tourism Management Perspectives* 37 (2021): 1–11, doi:10.1016/j.tmp.2020.100776.

Khan, Imad. "Why Animal Crossing Is the Game for the Coronavirus Moment." *The New York Times,* April 7, 2020.

legomasta99. "[Minecraft Computer Engineering] - Quad-Core Redstone Computer v5.0 [12k sub special!]." YouTube, December 29, 2018, https://www.youtube.com/watch?v=SbO0tqH8f5I.

MacDonald, Keza. "No Man's Sky Developer Sean Murray: 'It Was as Bad as Things Can Get'". *The Guardian,* July 20, 2018, https://www.theguardian.com/games/2018/jul/20/no-mans-sky-next-hello-games-sean-murray-harassment-interview.

McGonical, Jane. *Reality is Broken: Why Games Make us Better and How They Can Change the World.* London: Penguin, 2011.

Mojang Studios. *Minecraft.* Mojang Studios. Microsoft Windows. 2011.

Murray, Sean. "No Man's Sky." E3 PlayStation Press Conference, 2014.

Murray, Sean. "No Man's Sky Gameplay Trailer." E3 PlayStation Press Conference, 2015.

Nintendo EPD. *Animal Crossing: New Horizons.* Nintendo. Nintendo Switch. 2020.

Nye, David E. *American Technological Sublime.* Cambridge: MIT Press, 1996.

Obsidian Entertainment. *Grounded.* Xbox Game Studios. Microsoft Windows. 2022.

Ozimek, Adam. "Future Workforce Report 2021: How Remote Work is Changing Businesses Forever." *Upwork.com,* 2021, https://www.upwork.com/research/future-workforce-report.

Playrix. *Homescapes.* Playrix. iOs. 2017.

Reid, Erin. "Embracing, Passing, Revealing, and the Ideal Worker Image: How People Navigate Expected and Experienced Professional Identities." *Organization Science* 26, no. 4 (2015): 997–1017.

Studio Wildcard. *Ark: Survival Evolved.* Studio Wildcard. Microsoft Windows. 2017.

The Late Show With Steven Colbert. "Sean Murray May Have Replaced Morgan Freeman As God." YouTube, October 3, 2015, https://www.youtube.com/watch?v=ZqeN6hj4dZU.

Urry, John, and Jonas Larsen. *The Tourist Gaze 3.0.* London: Sage, 2011.

van Leeuwen, Bart. "If We Are Flâneurs, Can We Be Cosmopolitans?" *Urban Studies* 56, no. 2 (2019): 301–16, doi:10.1177/0042098017724120.

Wang, Vivian, and Zixu Wang. "In China, Young People Ditch Prestige Jobs for Manual Labor." *The New York Times,* April 11, 2023, https://www.nytimes.com/2023/04/11/world/asia/china-youth-employment.html.

Woldoff, Rachael A., and Robert C. Litchfield. *Digital Nomads*. Oxford: Oxford University Press, 2021.

Yee, Andrew Z. H., and Jeremy R. H. Sng. "Animal Crossing and COVID-19: A Qualitative Study Examining How Video Games Satisfy Basic Psychological Needs During the Pandemic." *Frontiers in Psychology* 13 (2022): 1–13, doi:10.3389/fpsyg.2022.800683.

Zynga. *Farmville*. Zynga. iOS. 2009.

6 When Here Becomes There

In the previous chapters I have mostly been focusing on games that take their players to fictional realms they cannot physically visit. In this final chapter, I want to return to games that, like Assassin's Creed, are about planet Earth. Particularly, I will focus on the extent to which our planet can be made accessible, or escape our reach, when presented in ludic and digitized form. How do different corporeal and vehicular modalities allow us to engage with our planet? How does the planet appear or disappear—and how is it domesticated and essentialized—as we traverse it? Several of the themes I have been discussing in previous chapters will return here: particularly, the pivotal role of work in appropriating the planet, and the capacity of digital media to overwhelm the imagination. I also want to touch upon the rise of mixed realities through AR and VR experiences, which introduces issues of sensorimotor approximation, as well as opportunities for accessibility and inclusion.

Pedestrian Gamification

The first type of movement I want to discuss is pedestrian; the kind that, ostensibly, brings us closest to the world. While I have already discussed walking simulators in Chapter 4, I here want to turn to the massively popular location-based AR games released by Niantic Labs. The most popular example is *Pokémon Go*,[1] originally released in 2016 but still remarkably popular in 2023. The game can be considered a mediated version of treasure hunting, or hide and seek.[2]

Pokémon Go uses mobile devices with GPS to locate, capture, train, and battle the titular creatures, which appear on your phone screen as though they are out there on the street. The game borrows from concepts developed in geocaching, an outdoor treasure-hunting game using GPS-enabled devices. "Geocachers" navigate to a specific set of GPS coordinates and then attempt to find a container with a note or small trinket hidden at that location.

In *Pokémon Go*, these containers are swapped out for virtual Pokémon. There are just over 700 of them to catch, with more being added across the game's updates. The game features some region-exclusive Pokémon, also known as regional Pokémon, which are only available in specific geographical areas. You must physically visit these locations to catch the Pokémon, and this has led many people to explore new cities, parks, and tourist attractions.

As a result, *Pokémon Go* has become a popular tool for promoting tourism in different regions and cities. Niantic Labs has organized various real-life events and meet-ups since the game's launch, such as the annual Pokémon Go Fest. These events offer enhanced in-game rewards for the attendees and often are developed in collaboration with local entities or governmental bodies, incentivizing players to explore a city or park. The larger gatherings attract player counts ranging from thousands to as many as two million participants in a single event. During the events, rare Pokémon variants and items will appear more frequently, and players can engage in special trades.

The events introduce a kind of tourism that is dependent on the symbolic value of the game, with the space itself forming the backdrop. Some have argued that as a result, the game produces a sense of belonging by facilitating conversations between strangers with similar passion for the game.[3] While the game brings otherwise individuated tourists together, it is a very narrow type of "belonging." It is a niche motive for visiting a place, and it allows us to reflect on the idea of commonality in tourism. We may visit the same places, but we are so often segregated based on our goals and backgrounds.

While the fostering of these player connections may be commended, the effects are unclear. A 2019 empirical study hypothesized that the frequent connectedness with strangers when playing *Pokémon Go* may lead to increased empathy, but found no significant effects.[4] What's more: these connections also develop along thoroughly established socio-economic lines. It is worth remembering that "automated" computational systems often integrate or even exacerbate existing social divisions and hierarchies in their models. For instance, the design of *Pokémon Go* reinforces existing geographically-linked biases,[5] as players in urban areas and neighborhoods with smaller minority populations were able to find a more diverse range of Pokémon. The game thus incentivizes movement towards these advantaged areas and away from rural ones.

AR games such as *Pokémon Go* also raise questions about "immersion" and our attention to the world around us. *Pokémon Go* features an "AR mode," which uses the camera and gyroscope on the player's mobile device to display an image of a Pokémon as though it were standing around on the street. Playing the game with this mode means looking around the streets not to focus on the streets, but on everything that is projected onto them. The reduced environmental awareness while playing the AR game led respondents of a field study to report near misses or actual collisions with an object in their environment while playing (see Figure 6.1).

Existing research has tended to focus on the impact of *Pokémon Go* on physical activity, and whether the game increases the number of daily steps players take.[6] But as a means to motivate travel, it also prompts other questions.

When Here Becomes There 89

Figure 6.1 The AR mode of *Pokémon Go*. Author screenshot.

What kind of walking is this? When a player is emotionally invested in catching Pokémon, what does engagement with place look like?

These questions loom large in the history of subversive urban walking, which is oriented toward the ways in which space can be approached in a purposeless manner. A notable example is the psychogeographic approach of the Situationist International, which reached its apex during the late 1960s. As I discussed in Chapter 4, the revolutionary artistic movement engaged in aimless wandering, which they called *dérive*: an occupation of urban spaces that aims to reclaim these spaces from commercial exploitation as sites for social interaction, leisure, and civic engagement.

The need for such critical rethinking has not decreased. Commercial messaging in the form of billboards, digital displays, and sponsored installations is prevalent in parks, public squares, and transportation hubs. There is a continued proliferation of privately-owned public spaces,[7] and urban redevelopment projects that prioritize commercial activities like shopping and dining. Games such as *Pokémon Go* are an extension of these approaches, and offer a glimpse into a future of individuated commercial relations to place. Instead of inscribing business interests into the cityscape, it envisions these interests as a personalized *overlay* by which our planet can be reimagined as a repository of virtual assets.

This means an intensification of commercial potential. As a prime example of pedestrian gamification, *Pokémon Go* demonstrates the fluid boundaries of the magic circle of play. As long as you are walking, you might as well be playing. The phone in your pocket is a constant reminder that there might be something new to do, some task to complete. It is here that the forms of "inhabiting" a virtual space and the kinds of low-effort work that foster engagement (as demonstrated in Chapter 5) escape from the screen and permeate physical space. The kinds of menial labor that make games such as Animal Crossing so immersive are brought to the street.

The game thus effectively overwrites public spaces. *Pokémon Go* is a game that does not subvert one's view of the environment. It does not enable us to see our environment anew; in a sense, it makes us not see it at all. The player's journey is controlled by the game's algorithm and the placement of PokéStops and Gyms. Rather than encouraging a deeper engagement with these spaces and their cultural or historical significance, it recontextualizes them as waypoints. *Pokémon Go* does not as much project the game onto the physical world as the other way around.

Of course, alternatives to this approach are conceivable. Many cities offer AR walking tours for participants to see virtual reconstructions of destroyed buildings, learn about historical events that took place, or be informed about landmarks. Games have a similar capacity to include the world in their scope; to give just a simple example, histories and particularities of place could be used to raise questions about the presence, or absence, of certain Pokémon. But the planet is kept at a distance. Scrutinizing the pavement or the park for Pokémon through one's phone, one might wonder: where is the pavement? Where is the park?

And yet, while *Pokémon Go* keeps the world at a distance from the player, it ties the player to the world through geolocation. *Pokémon Go*'s location permission lets the game track where you are, how long you have been there, and what kinds of events are going on during gameplay. Niantic can also use this information to show players ads for businesses in that area. The developer might well be able to display a map to visualize all the game's players on it—a bit like the Pokémon they are gathering. It is a map that is part of a bigger game of surveillance technology; one that keeps track of us as we keep track of our collection.

Racing Through Utopia

Next, I want to turn to a video game that focuses on vehicular interaction: the thrill-oriented travel of the Forza Horizon series, produced by Playground Games. The series fuses motorsport simulation and open-world exploration:

unlike traditional racing games where players are bound to a track, the Forza Horizon series encourages exploration of its world. You can participate in all manner of events, such as traditional circuit races, point-to-point sprints, and off-road escapades.

The central premise and narrative backdrop for the series is the so-called "Horizon Festival," portrayed as a joyous celebration of cars, music, and freedom. Recent entries open with the player-character driving towards the center of the festival, complete with high-energy crowds, low-flying planes, and fireworks.

The latest installment in the series, *Forza Horizon 5*,[8] is set in an abstracted, dreamlike version of Mexico. Like other contemporary race games, the game looks almost photorealistic; its claim to immersion is largely based on its graphical fidelity. The game map includes beaches, jungles, deserts, and mountains, and squeezes the country's diverse geography into just a few dozen square miles. There is a conscious effort to frame the game as a travelogue, complete with scenic routes and picturesque panoramas. Radio stations in the game play a mix of popular hits and traditional Mexican music, which are regularly drowned out by the roar of your engine.

Forza Horizon 5's essentialized Mexican world is a sanitized and strictly vehicular world. The only pedestrians to be seen are festival spectators, standing behind unbreakable barricades. Anywhere else in town, the sidewalks are empty. The lack of pedestrians is one of the ways in which the game avoids any sense of danger or physical consequence to its high-speed automotive sports (see Figure 6.2).

Figure 6.2 Empty sidewalks in *Forza Horizon 5*. Author screenshot.

Obstacles in the game world are either impervious or insubstantial. Trees, fences, and rocks can be driven through at will, breaking apart on contact. A more robust house or wall will lead your car to crash, stop, and take cosmetic damage—but there is no concept of harm, let alone fatality. Other cars on the road can be crashed against, but they are similarly indestructible. Their windows are blinded, and their drivers are hidden from view.

In other words, the game's graphical fidelity has to do with its essentialization of Mexico-by-car. Not only are machines easier to computationally render than people, the scenery is made to look impressive especially when speeding through it at a breakneck pace. As insulating and distancing devices, cars separate the tourist from the lived reality of the locations they pass through. The Forza Horizon series is built on a hyperactive and impersonal tourist gaze; one that views its exotic locations through an exceptionally glossy lens, and that aims to cycle as fast as possible through all kinds of spectacular locations. The game's title screen itself is a montage of moving postcards of the country's radically diverse landscapes, set to a smooth Mexican-tinged soundtrack.

While there are factual places in *Forza Horizon 5*, they are easter eggs, hidden away to be recognized by players familiar with Mexico. They include the Riviera Maya, Teotihuacán, and Mulegé. None of these places are placed on the map where they are in reality; this game is not set in Mexico, but in a dream of Mexican-ness. The game reminds the player at all times not to reflect on its mechanics and systems: the game's radio host and voiceover repeatedly tell you not to worry about these systems but to "have fun." The game also hands out experience points (XP) for a wide range of player actions in the world: speeding, drifting, near-misses, crashing, and so on. These activities are so ubiquitous that the XP meter is always going up, almost passively, yielding a constant feed of visual feedback that motivates play.

The game, despite its renderings of some Mexican places, has little to do with the country itself. In fact, it demonstrates well how the "topography of utopia is now projected into the space of the *virtual*," as sociologist Majid Yar has argued.[9] While Yar mostly focuses on the Internet, I would argue that games are symptomatic of the tendency to imagine utopia as an ontologically "Other" space, separate from the "Real." The world as seen through the lens of Forza Horizon is one without any issues because its only people are radio DJs announcing the next song or in-game event.

Tourism, Forza Horizon reminds us, allows people to engage with foreign environments in a relatively consequence-free way. They can leave whenever they want, and they are rarely held responsible for any long-term impacts of their visit. This series revels in this logic of unaccountable gazing, to the point where it is about a country on Planet Earth in name only. It transforms its countries so thoroughly that the only thing that remains of them is their capacity to be viewed from a distance, as a stereotypically superficial tourist. Its continued popularity, meanwhile, demonstrates just how pervasively *fun* such hollow touristic interactions can be—and indeed, how difficult it may prove to move beyond them.

Keep it Professional

So how *can* games go beyond the tourist gaze? Perhaps the most common way, discussed in Chapter 5, is through a sense of purpose through work. Here, I want to connect that logic to simulation games that take place on our planet, and that further blur the relationship between "players" and "characters." In *Euro Truck Simulator 2*[10] (*ETS2*), you work as an HGV driver delivering goods throughout Europe. The primary objective of the game is to transport various types of cargo between cities across the continent while adhering to real-world traffic rules and regulations. As players progress through the game, they can expand their trucking empire by acquiring new trucks, employing drivers, and managing a fleet of vehicles.

Gameplay in *ETS2* begins with the player creating a profile and choosing a starting city from a list of locations in Europe. You are then handed a basic truck and a small amount of money, and is put in the driver's seat to begin your career as a truck driver. As is common for the simulator genre, this career is emphatically your own. In the game's third-person mode, you can only see a vague outline of a player-character behind the tinted truck windows, and there is no way to look at your own reflection in the rear-view mirror.

Initially, you must take on quick jobs, which involve transporting cargo using a truck provided by the employer. These jobs offer a fixed reward upon successful completion, with expenses such as fuel and tolls being covered by the employer. As you complete jobs and accumulate money, you can eventually purchase your own trucks. With your own vehicle, you can accept freight market jobs, where you become responsible for covering fuel costs and other expenses. These jobs typically offer higher rewards, allowing you to grow your trucking business more quickly.

Unlike most other vehicle-oriented games, being a professional means that traffic laws must be obeyed: players must maintain appropriate speeds, stop at red lights, yield to other vehicles, and back up their trucks into tight parking areas. Players are also responsible for monitoring their truck's fuel, tire wear, and overall condition, as well as adhering to regulated rest periods to avoid driver fatigue. *ETS2* even features an economic simulation component, allowing players to expand their trucking business by purchasing garages, hiring additional drivers, and managing a fleet of trucks. As players progress, they can upgrade their vehicles with new parts and accessories, improving their performance and fuel efficiency. *ETS2* revolves around the same sense of ownership over place that I have been discussing throughout this book; here, however, it is an entrepreneurial instead of a touristic expansionism.

ETS2 offers a condensed network of European roads and highways. The representation of its cities, towns, and rural areas is similarly abbreviated; but unlike in games built on the tourist gaze, such as Assassin's Creed, here they are emptied of their touristic value. For instance, the typical landmarks of Paris are dropped in favor of a featureless recruitment agency, a bus station, a handful of commercial centers and hotels, and a construction area ironically titled Bâtisse—a usually slightly derogatory way to name any unremarkable building. These sites are decidedly functional: you can sleep in a hotel or drop off cargo at a construction site. There are no pedestrians on the streets, there is no life in the urban centers. The version of Europe in *ETS2* is strictly rendered through the professional gaze of truck operation (see Figure 6.3).

As the French anthropologist Marc Augé would have it, all of these environments are "non-places": they are defined primarily by their function, rather than by their cultural or historical significance. Augé points to malls, supermarkets, highways, and airports to argue that non-places are "non-relational" in that they do not allow for the development of meaningful social interactions, but instead involve interactions between people and institutions such as airports, airlines, companies, traffic police, and so on.[11]

Non-places allow visitors to engage with texts, not landscapes. Augé gives the example of the autoroute: "Main roads no longer pass through towns, but lists of their notable features—and, indeed, a whole commentary—appear on big signboards nearby. In a sense, the traveller is absolved of the need to stop or even look."[12] Removed from the intimacy of everyday life, these roads, railroads, and airline routes push the solitary traveler to leaf through a magazine instead of focusing on local details and lived realities. Augé calls it a "contractual relationship" in which tickets, passports, visas, and credit cards replace identity with the purely functional role of being a passenger.[13]

ETS2 places these liminal spaces in the center of attention through the lens of professionalism and *hard work*. In doing so, it defamiliarizes players from the common inattention that Augé points out. The fun in *ETS2* comes from injecting these spaces with a sense of purpose that is normally only reserved for those who travel the roads of Europe for their jobs. It activates a range of

Figure 6.3 Paris in *Euro Truck Simulator 2*. Author screenshot.

signifiers that we normally disregard. This results in an attentiveness to these "textual" sites *as* landscapes, which are worth noticing.

ETS2 invites players to enact a professional relation to place. You are not traveling across the European map for fun, but because it is your job. It is this focus on work that connects the games in this chapter to those discussed in Chapter 5. But where the work in survival games such as *Minecraft* and *Grounded* is a de-escalated affair—a series of chores punctuating elements of combat and survival—*ETS2* is entirely about one's profession. It is just as much an economic sandbox as it is a world sandbox: blue-collar work can through effort become a lucrative business. In fact, labor itself becomes the primary form of legitimization for the player's claim to space. It means to say: "I belong here because I'm working here."

There is a productive contrast between these simulator games and the "life simulators" such as Animal Crossing discussed in the previous chapter. Whereas I argued that these games are about lowering the stakes of work, *ETS2* produces a touristic gaze that is always also a non-touristic gaze. It is precisely *not* about feeling "at home," or about building a community; it is about belonging on the road because you are busy, in the sense that you are *owning a business*. The only ultimate sense of belonging the player has is towards their entrepreneurial stakes. This creates a stringent commercial sense of forward momentum, of continuous expansion and "pushing things forward" that renders the textual landscape as something less aesthetic and more transient. These truck stops and hotels might perhaps best be approached from a framework of *atmospheres*.

Philosopher Gernot Böhme defines atmospheres as the emotional tones or moods prevalent in a specific location or region. They are not localized within an individual or object but emerge from the interaction of both. Böhme writes how "atmospheres are a typical intermediate phenomenon, something between subject and object," lacking a "secure ontological status."[14] That is, the perceiving subject itself also adds to the emerging atmosphere.[15] This affective perspective makes it clear that the sites in *ETS2* are not so much places, but nodes in a network of entrepreneurial activity. The player approaches these sites with a restless attitude. Each site is a stop amid the perpetual sluggish motion of the truck. This not only abolishes place but also *puts everything into place*: that is, it allows the player to see the infrastructural connections between arterial roads, the relations between suburbs and city centers, and the approximate distance between European metropolises. *ETS2* brings the world closer insofar as it offers a means to work in it.

Elective Alienation

The third and final modality I want to discuss here is that of flight; the modern technological wonder of seeing the planet from a cruising altitude of 35,000 feet. For an emblematic example, we can look at Microsoft Flight Simulator.

The first version in the series, *FS1 Flight Simulator*,[16] was first released in 1980 for the Apple II. It was created by subLOGIC, a company that specialized in flight simulation software. The game's scenery included 36 tiles in a 6-by-6 pattern, translating to a few hundred square kilometers, and one airplane. A review in science fiction magazine *The Space Gamer* ended on a high note: "All things considered, this is the single most impressive computer game I have seen. It creates a whole new standard."[17]

Throughout the years, the series has continued to garner positive reviews. A review on gaming website IGN of the latest entry in the series, *Microsoft Flight Simulator 2020*[18] (*MFS*), starts off with a superlative: "Microsoft Flight Simulator is the most incredible experience I've ever had on a computer." I find the hyperbolic language around these games quite revealing. There is something about the technological marvel of aviation that we normally only experience as tourists. When rendered through an interactive medium, it gives us a freedom of control that stands in sharp contrast with the passive experience of watching the world scroll by from behind a passenger window.

What *FS1 Flight Simulator* and *MFS* have in common is that both were able, in their own technological context, to model not just the intricacies of aviation but also the world below. In that sense, viewing *MFS* as a simulator of flight mechanics is reductive; it simulates the planet many players will be used to seeing from up high, defamiliarized at high altitudes. The feeling of disorientation or detachment experienced in airplanes is known as "aerial dissociation." When we are on the ground, we rely on visual and physical cues to make sense of our surroundings. In an airplane, these cues are missing or distorted. Humans and cars are invisible; mountains and skyscrapers are textures on the terrain. From this height, the earth is unanchored from the scale of human affairs. It is abstracted—but without the boundaries traced by maps. It reveals itself as a contiguous landscape.

The gaze that is being activated is planetary; an overview of *all* the cities, mountain ranges, and oceans you have seen passing by in transit. The game folds all of those places into one representative compendium. To recreate this version of Earth, the developers of *MFS* used machine learning to fill out most of the map by training it on tons upon tons of satellite photos. The developers partnered with Blackshark.ai, who developed a solution that uses Microsoft Azure and AI to analyze map data and photogrammetry to generate photorealistic 3D models of buildings, trees, terrain, and so on (see Figure 6.4). The AI drew much of the world from that data, with guidance from the developers. In addition, the game comes with two petabytes of satellite and high-altitude photography that can be streamed to your computer to accurately represent places around the world.

This results in a sense of control that is antonymous to the feeling you get in an airport terminal watching all of the other destinations flip by on a large screen. As Marc Augé wrote, airports are symbolized by excessive information.[19] They offer an overabundance of signifiers that commonly give rise to

When Here Becomes There 97

Figure 6.4 Paris in *Microsoft Flight Simulator 2020*. Author screenshot.

the wish you could swap out your destination for another one—or that you could visit all of them.

Playing *MFS* means to lean into that wish. The game boots up into a dashboard where the player can select to go into flight training, challenges, or a world map. The map is a model of our planet, silently suspended against a starry backdrop. Zooming in, you can select any airport in the world to depart from. With the click of a button, you are flying over sites you once visited or wanted to visit, cities you grew up in or fell in love in, places you think back on regularly, and places you simply forgot about.

Tellingly, the dials you are in control of are not just airplane controls, but planetary controls. Players can dial in the weather, calendar date, or time of day of their choice—but the game is synced up with real-time weather conditions, live air traffic, and current time. Launching into a flight with these real-time parameters yields a sensation of a continuous and immediate now-ness that seems typically modern in that it highlights the accelerated pace of existence. It brings to mind all of the planes taking off and landing and all of the cars on the highway in the present moment. It allows you to reflect on the global fact of simultaneity. It is telling, in that context, that *MFS* was released during the coronavirus pandemic. Its popularity is no doubt related to the restrictions its players were experiencing in their everyday life. The pandemic dramatically curtailed international travel, grounding flights and closing borders, while giving rise to stay-at-home orders and work-from-home protocols. With the world effectively off-limits, *MFS* provided a virtual window into viewing it.

As a flight simulator, *MFS* also closely models the tactile experience of aviation, including the knobs, dials, and buttons of its dashboard that can be viewed in first person. The player does not simply jump into a flight without trouble: *MFS* requires you to learn flight controls, the basics of navigation, stability, traffic patterns, and so on. In the aforementioned IGN Review, Seth Macy notes: "This is the first game I've ever played where I downloaded a PDF manual from a real-world piece of equipment to reference during play—and everything in the manual checks out to the virtual hardware."[20]

In other words, *MFS* is a game of virtual sightseeing, but it is also about dexterity; about successfully taking off and landing a plane on a runway. Learning to fly a virtual jet is not without its challenges. Becoming familiar with the controls and with different aircraft will lead players to frequently crash into that many-colored marble that, for anyone except a stunt pilot, is better kept at a distance.

Upon the game's release, players immediately began searching for and practicing their taxiing skills on particularly dangerous airfields, such as Tenzing-Hillary Airport in Nepal and Barra Airport in Scotland. While many of these airstrips are located in beautiful settings, the skills required to fly there demand focus. Players must stabilize their aircraft and navigate routes while managing fuel consumption and other real-world concerns.

When these skill-based tasks are handled and the player is on cruise control, what is simulated is a very particular perspective on the planet: one in which the physicality and immediacy of the landscape are transmuted into a shifting tableau of colors, textures, and patterns, with little resemblance to the tapestry of life unfolding below. At cruising altitude, the minutiae of the earth's surface are obscured, with entire cities, ecosystems, and cultures reduced to indistinguishable shapes. Being a flight passenger means a heightened sense of temporality and transience, with each passing moment bringing you closer to your destination. Boarding an aircraft and settling into your assigned seat, you are effectively isolated from those around you, retreating into your own private world of entertainment, work, and contemplation.

Being a tourist means craving a kind of modern planetary dissociation. *MFS*'s popularity during the pandemic invites comparisons to the temporary popularity of "flights to nowhere," which offered passengers the opportunity to experience air travel without leaving their home countries.[21] Qantas, for instance, offered a seven-hour sightseeing flight over Queensland and the Gold Coast, New South Wales, and the country's remote outback heartlands, which sold out in just 10 minutes in September 2020. These flights provided a brief respite from the monotony of lockdowns and travel restrictions, allowing passengers to briefly regain a sense of dissociative normalcy.

MFS offers a familiar engagement with the world through a window. It presents that world as a "distant planet that seems strangely suspended from the chaos of sociality and life."[22] The immediate physicality of travel is replaced by a controlled, sanitized environment where the act of travel becomes more a journey of the mind and imagination than of the body. Our minds are free to wander, to imagine where we are going, and to connect what we see to our past experiences or future plans. We conjure up images of our destination, recall similar landscapes from past journeys, or dream about future adventures. Imaginative travel practically becomes more significant than the actual travel we are engaging in. This particularly modern capacity to associate with the world through dissociation leads me to my final example: *Google Earth VR.*

It's All in Your Mind

In the fall of 2016, Google released a virtual reality version of Google Earth for Valve's gaming platform Steam, *Google Earth VR*.[23] Based on the Google Earth app, it allows users to explore a three-dimensional digital representation of the Earth, with all its landscapes, cities, and natural wonders. Using satellite imagery and 3D modeling technology, the app allows users to visit any location on Earth, view it from different angles, and manipulate time and weather conditions.

Google Earth VR offers no gameplay, no challenges—just a silent, frozen image of our planet. To play is to be caught in a temporary version of the world, set apart from reality and yet exploring a realm that has been fully modeled on it. It is not a game in the traditional sense of the word, but you do play it. You have the freedom and autonomy to zoom out and spin the world around as you would with a globe, then zoom in and swerve over the landscape. You can travel to metropolitan areas, flying in between roughly rendered skyscrapers, and then, remembering where you lived ten years ago, hover over a suburb half a world away, squinting to see whether you recognize your old building, or if eucalyptus trees still line the street.

Google Earth VR offers more than the promise that *you can go there*. It completes the transformation of "here" into "there"—that is, it presents a model of the world we inhabit, and enables a type of imagination that leads from place to place, from memory to travel fantasy. If we think about it as a rhetorical device, it is a polysyndeton, a succession of coordinating conjunctions that emphasizes the equal importance of every item in the series. You can travel to Bali *and* Rio, to New York *and* Hong Kong *and* the house where your grandmother used to live. The lack of any physical restrictions, like the ones in *MFS*, enables this succession to play out at pace. There's a smooth zoom effect as you move towards and away from the globe, seeing it intermittently at eye level and as a ball suspended in space.

Google Earth's image of the world, in short, "shares with Spaceship Earth something of the quality of a fetish, a shimmering image meant to be consumed, perhaps as an icon of nostalgia for an Earth we may be about to lose."[24] It offers the viewer the right angles to aesthetically appreciate an otherwise unimaginable object, transforming it from something we live in, to something we can read. Still, this text is marked by imperfections: moving too close to the earth transmutes the surface into a patchwork of smudgy textures and frozen polygonal objects. These imperfections are, for now, an inevitable product of the programmatic attempt to transform satellite images into 3D renditions.

Yet, this VR experience seems most clearly to epitomize a type of model that is in its infancy. It may be a precursor to the inevitable future in the metaverse awaiting us all. Whether that future is led by Meta, Apple, Google, Amazon, or anyone else, this potential of a map overlapping the territory feels less inconceivable than it once did. The technology is not yet sophisticated enough to be satisfactorily convincing, but it seems to draw closer by the day.

Notes

1 Niantic, *Pokémon Go.*
2 Cord, Roeßiger, and Schwarz, "Geocaching Data as an Indicator," 152.
3 Vella et al., "A Sense of Belonging," 283.
4 Alloway et al., "Gotta Catch 'Em All."
5 Colley et al., "The geography of Pokémon GO," 1179.
6 E.g. Khamzina et al., "Impact of Pokémon Go on Physical Activity."
7 See for instance NYC Planning, "New York City's Privately Owned Public Places."
8 Playground Games, *Forza Horizon 5.*
9 Yar, "Virtual Utopias and Dystopias," 179.
10 SCS Software, *Euro Truck Simulator 2.*
11 Augé, *Non-Places,* 96.
12 Augé, *Non-Places,* 97.
13 Augé, *Non-Places,* 101–2.
14 Böhme, *The Aesthetics of Atmospheres,* 29.
15 Zimmerman and Huberts, "From Walking Simulator," 32.
16 Sublogic, *FS1 Flight Simulator.*
17 Mishcon, "Capsule Reviews," 28.
18 Asobo Studio, *Microsoft Flight Simulator.*
19 Augé, *Non-Places,* 109.
20 Macy, "Microsoft Flight Simulator Review."
21 Street, "Flights to Nowhere."
22 Munster, *An Aesthesia of Networks,* 46.
23 Google, *Google Earth VR.*
24 Helmreich, "From Spaceship Earth to Google Ocean," 1219.

References

Alloway, Tracy Packiam, and Rachel Carpenter. "'Gotta Catch 'Em All'—Can Playing Pokémon Go Influence Mood and Empathy?" *Game Studies* 19, no. 2 (2019).

Asobo Studio. *Microsoft Flight Simulator.* Xbox Game Studios. Microsoft Windows. 2020.

Augé, Marc. *Non-Places: An Introduction to Supermodernity.* New York: Verso Books, 2020.

Böhme, Gernot. *The Aesthetics of Atmospheres,* edited by Jean-Paul Thibaud. London: Routledge, 2017.

Colley, Ashley, Jacob Thebault-Spieker, Allen Yilun Lin, Donald Degraen, Benjamin Fischman, Jonna Häkkilä, Kate Kuehl, Valentina Nisi, Nuno Jardim Nunes, Nina Wenig, Dirk Wenig, Brent Hecht, and Johannes Schöning. "The Geography of Pokémon GO: Beneficial and Problematic Effects on Places and Movement."

Conference on Human Factors in Computing Systems Proceedings (May 2017): 1179–92, doi:10.1145/3025453.3025495.

Cord, Anna, Franz Roeßiger, and Nina Schwarz. "Geocaching Data as an Indicator for Recreational Ecosystem Services in Urban Areas: Exploring Spatial Gradients, Preferences and Motivations." *Landscape and Urban Planning* 144 (2015): 151–62, doi:10.1016/j.landurbplan.2015.08.015.

De Greef, Lilian, Meredith Morris, and Kori Inkpen. "TeleTourist: Immersive Telepresence Tourism for Mobility-Restricted Participants." *Proceedings of the 19th ACM Conference on Computer Supported Cooperative Work and Social Computing Companion* (2016): 273–76.

Google. *Google Earth VR*. Google. Microsoft Windows. 2016.

Helmreich, Stefan. "From Spaceship Earth to Google Ocean: Planetary Icons, Indexes, and Infrastructures." *Social Research* 78, no. 4 (2011): 1211–42.

Jacobs, Jane. *The Death and Life of Great American Cities*. New York: Random House, 1961.

Khamzina, Madina, Kaustubh V. Parab, Ruopeng An, Tiffany Bullard, and Diana S. Grigsby-Toussaint. "Impact of Pokémon Go on Physical Activity: A Systematic Review and Meta-Analysis." *American Journal of Preventive Medicine* 58, no. 2 (2020): 270–82.

Macy, Seth G. "Microsoft Flight Simulator Review." *IGN*, August 17, 2020, https://www.ign.com/articles/microsoft-flight-simulator-review.

Mishcon, J. "Capsule Reviews." *The Space Gamer*. Steve Jackson Games 31, 1980.

Munster, Anna. *An Aesthesia of Networks: Conjunctive Experience in Art and Technology*. Cambridge: MIT Press, 2013.

Niantic. *Pokémon Go*. Niantic. iOS. 2016.

NYC Planning. "New York City's Privately Owned Public Places." NYC.org, https://www.nyc.gov/site/planning/plans/pops/pops-history.page.

Pinder, David. *Visions of the City: Utopianism, Power and Politics in Twentieth-Century Urbanism*. Edinburgh: Edinburgh University Press, 2005.

Playground Games. *Forza Horizon 5*. Xbox Game Studios. Microsoft Windows. 2021.

SCS Software. *Euro Truck Simulator 2*. SCS Software. Microsoft Windows. 2012.

Street, Francesca. "Flights to Nowhere Changed Covid-era Air Travel. This is Where They're Headed Now." *CNN Travel*, January 26, 2022, https://www.cnn.com/travel/article/flight-to-nowhere-future/index.html.

Sublogic. *FS1 Flight Simulator*. Sublogic. Apple II. 1980.

Upadhayaya, Pranil. "Sustainability Threats to Mountain Tourism with Tourist Mechanized Mobility Induced Global Warming: A Case Study of Nepal." *Journal of Tourism and Hospitality* 4, no. 2 (2015): 1–7.

Vella, Kellie, Daniel Johnson, Vanessa Cheng, Tracey Davenport, Jo Mitchell, Madison Klarkowski, and Cody Phillips. "A Sense of Belonging: Pokémon GO and Social Connectedness." *Games and Culture* 14, no. 6 (2019): 583–603, doi:10.1177/1555412017719973.

Yar, Majid. "Virtual Utopias and Dystopias–The Cultural Imaginary of the Internet." In *Utopia: Social Theory and the Future*, edited by Michael Hviid Jacobsen and Keith Tester, 179–95. London: Routledge, 2016.

Zimmerman, Felix, and Christian Huberts. "From Walking Simulator to Ambience Action Game: A Philosophical Approach to a Misunderstood Genre." *Press Start* 2, no. 2 (2019): 29–50.

7 Conclusion

In May 2023, Nintendo released a commercial for *The Legend of Zelda: Tears of the Kingdom*[1] (*TOTK*). The ad starts with a middle-aged white man in a suit, on the bus, heading to work. He looks like a successful businessman, but he has a resigned look on his face. His life looks like a repetition of monotonous commutes; his flourishing career has smothered the spark of adventure. When he arrives at his luxurious walk-up apartment after a long day of work, he notices a copy of the latest Zelda title on his kitchen counter.

A smile appears on his face. We see the businessman playing around in the game, which allows players to cobble together vehicles and tools from objects in the game world. He builds a raft to sail across a pond. He fights off a boss, holding back a squeal of delight on his next commute. He steers Link around on a plane glider, soaring high in the sky. The man sighs contentedly—and then looks outside at the field and the clear blue sky through his bus window. It seems as though he is seeing it for the first time.

The game's advertisement acknowledges the facts about its player base. More adults engage in video games than children. This is a commercial written for a generation of players who have grown up with the Zelda series; who might have marveled at the grand adventures of *Ocarina of Time* as twelve-year-olds and now have successful careers and children of their own. The ad speaks to something akin to a midlife crisis: it promises the thrill of adventure for those having to manage jobs, families, and retirement savings plans.

It is all the more interesting, then, that *TOTK* is all about the kind of work I discussed in Chapter 5. The game, built on the same engine and taking place on the same map as its predecessor, *Breath of the Wild*, is in many ways a reshuffling of places and encounters. However, the novel focus in *TOTK* is on the building mechanics, fusing items and objects in the world in order to create contraptions and navigate through the game in creative ways. Like *Breath of the Wild* before it, the game encourages players to experiment and find creative solutions to problems. The game's creators refer to this as "multiplicative gameplay": the more tools and mechanics that players have at their disposal, the more possibilities there are for individualized gameplay experiences.

What is also multiplied is the content that people can share about these experiences. *TOTK* is a "single-player game" in name only; the whole

DOI: 10.4324/9781003404590-7

package is geared towards sharing, towards *let's play* videos on streaming platforms, and toward top-10 highlight reels on YouTube. It is a game with a lot of content, in order for players to create even more. Perhaps *TOTK* signals something about the future of the open-world game: as in tourism, people might want to experience things not so much intrinsically, but in order to share it with others. It might not be about *you can go there*, but about *you can post this*.

What should also be highlighted about the advertisement is that the middle-aged professional is rediscovering his inner child not just because of a sense of exploration, but because of his rekindled creativity amidst the predictable pathways of middle-class life. The commercial shows that the ideology of exploration, the promise that *you can go there*, is most effective when it does not revolve around magnitude alone, but when it allows us to be defamiliarized toward the world around us. It promises that you will see the most ordinary farmland on your ride to work with new eyes.

Key Themes

The main focus of this book has been the concept of defamiliarization: the capacity to unsettle the player/tourist and allow them to rethink their own subjectivities in late modern society. I have argued that such subversive strategies are necessary, as the catchphrase *you can go there*, and its different permutations are potentially exploitative. The "you" commonly refers to the tourist who is enticed into forms of play that enact the tourist gaze, and who is nudged away from reflection and subversion. My investigation has led to the discussion of three dominant themes.

The first theme is *control*. The tourist gaze, both in video games and outside of them, is one that originates in a dominant subjecting consciousness and projects itself to be fundamentally free. In reality, it is often controlled by a wide range of interlocking systems and infrastructures that accommodate tourist experiences. Games provide the opportunity to reflect on those systems. I used examples such as *Outer Wilds* to highlight the tactile interfaces and locomotive affordances that allow players to rub up against the world they are placed in. Touristic defamiliarization, as a form of virtually embodied interaction, means reorienting yourself towards the impression of control—both its limits and its subversive capacity.

The second theme is *scale*. Games exemplify a long-standing fascination with the sublime in tourism: many of them are explicitly modeled so that players may enter into and interact with Friedrich's famous painting. I noted how the promise of sublime experience can bite back and lead to disappointment, evidenced by the response to *No Man's Sky*. But games can do more than simply copy the sublime aesthetic. They can introduce it to complicate it—for instance, through the detail-oriented curiosity of *The Legend of Zelda: Breath of the Wild*.

The third theme is *work*. Games are both an extension of and a reaction against the intensification of labor under late capitalism. Travel is linguistically related to the French "travail," meaning labor; this is quite evident in many of the virtual environments we visit, where we perform all kinds of repetitive chores. Yet games do not just repeat the late capitalist mandate of passionately engaging with your work, or viewing it as an integral part of your life. I discussed how games like the Animal Crossing series reorient players toward these myths. The perennial criticism of time-intensive games as a "waste of time" is a classic case of projection; it is a tacit criticism of the types of work-oriented lives we have normalized.

To be clear, the act of defamiliarization in these games does not occur in spite of the act of touristic gazing—and neither is that gaze erased. Instead, games can utilize the tourist gaze and direct it towards the unique characteristics of what is being observed, in order to foreground them. As a result, games can absorb and exceed the preoccupations with which tourists and gamers arrive.

I hope this research inspires game designers to consider critically what type of tourist gaze they are hoping to foster—even if through subtle modifications. Discussing the concept of

"wandering" as a radically unproductive, contemplative, and anticapitalist form of play, Melissa Kagen has observed that "one can travel through a space in very different ways with only slightly altered affects. The valence is actually quite thin between the wanderer, the explorer, and the conqueror."[2]

The comparative view I took in this book underscores that point. The formal differences between sandbox games such as Assassin's Creed and recent entries in The Legend of Zelda series are limited. Yet, the specific ways in which control and scale are imagined yield significant differences: one encourages the player to gaze at the world as something to appropriate, the other subverts both its own sublime grandeur and its Arthurian quest by focusing on minutia. The player is diverted to the point of forgetting about their initial interest in the world as a space to be rescued and conquered.

It is within these kinds of choices about how spaces can be appropriated, and about our role as agents in a wider system, that I have located the capacity for defamiliarization from common touristic myths. It constitutes the difference between simply moving through a space, and *being moved* by it. With that, I mean more than just an affective response: games can counteract neoliberal phantasms of maximized productivity, and of the sovereign gazing subject—the *you* who simply *can go there*. Defamiliarization can offer players new insights about their place in symbolic systems that perpetuate power imbalances and inequalities. "Being moved" represents a powerful potential to change people's view of the world and their place in it. The *there*, ultimately, can modify the *you*.

That is not to say, however, that defamiliarization is simply a design feature. It is not the case that "some games subvert the tourist gaze and some do not." To unsettle yourself as a player/tourist requires conscious effort, and the themes I have discussed in this book are intended as self-reflexive questions as much as suggestions for game design. What can we do to move beyond our status as Homo Laborans?[3] Do we simply reiterate our obsession with the grandiose and the sublime, or do we allow ourselves to pay attention to the details of the world? When do we accept being controlled by algorithmic systems and myths, and how can we tease apart these systems?

There are valuable perspectives on games and tourism that I have not been able to cover here. They include the gendered nature of the tourist gaze, intercultural orientations towards travel and tourism (for instance, comparing Japanese and Western games, or focusing on the Global South), the continuing reliance on tropes about Otherness in game narratives, and the fixation on apocalyptic scenarios in the context of global environmental distress. All of these perspectives make it possible to further complicate the idea of the tourist gaze in gaming.

Rendering the unfamiliar familiar is, all too often, a matter of tapping into the well of ideology. Western culture is very familiar with power fantasies, with ownership and conquest, with boundless opportunity, and with having "the world at your feet." Defamiliarization, by contrast, has no ready-made figures of speech or mechanics to employ. Viktor Shklovsky's point was that defamiliarization means that art can disrupt our automatic perception and understanding of the world: he held art in high regard because this was not a trivial task. This is not just to say that games can be art—that has been obvious for a long time. It is to say that games, as one of the most influential cultural forces in Western culture, should be held to a similar standard.

Notes

1 Nintendo Australia, "Rediscover Your Sense of Adventure."
2 Kagen, *Wandering Games*, 15.
3 Arendt, *The Human Condition*.

References

Arendt, Hannah. *The Human Condition*. Chicago: University of Chicago Press, 2013.
Kagen, Melissa. *Wandering Games*. Cambridge: MIT Press, 2022.
Nintendo Australia. "Rediscover Your Sense of Adventure With The Legend of Zelda: Tears of the Kingdom." YouTube, May 8, 2023, https://www.youtube.com/watch?v=wIJODMsYbkc&ab_channel=NintendoAU.

Index

aesthetics 22, 26, 43–44, 53, 63–64
affordances 23, 25, 77
Airbnb 59, 82
Algorithms 7, 17, 25–26, 59, 70–73
alienation 20, 39, 65, 81, 95
Animal Crossing: New Horizons (videogame) 79–82
anti-tourism 36–37
Assassin's Creed (videogame) 31, 38
Assassin's Creed II (videogame) 32
Assassin's Creed: Brotherhood (videogame) 32
Assassin's Creed Discovery Tours (videogame) 33–36
Assasin's Creed Origins (videogame) 35
Assassin's Creed Unity (videogame) 32
Assassin's Creed Valhalla (videogame) 35
Augé, Marc 94, 96
augmented reality 88, 90
authenticity 5, 19, 24, 56, 62, 76

Barthes, Roland 13
Bartle, Richard 25
bullshit jobs 58
business 80–81, 90, 93, 95

capitalism 39, 56, 81, 104
Carroll, Lewis 16
cartography 36
Chess, Shira 24
childish games 6, 32, 103
choice 31, 35, 51, 57, 59, 97, 104
colonialism 16, 25, 40–42, 45, 53, 71

compression of game worlds 51, 54, 63
constructionism 13–14
control 17, 20–21, 24–25, 44, 47, 57, 59, 65, 71, 96–98, 103–5
coronavirus pandemic 19, 79, 98
cosmopolitan 81
creativity 20, 70, 75, 77–78, 83, 103
crowds 36–39, 91
cryptocurrency 19
Csikszentmihalyi, Mihaly 19–20

Dear Esther (videogame) 52–53
death 39, 54, 55
decision-making 17
defamiliarization 23, 26–27, 43, 46, 65, 73–74, 94, 96, 103–5
Defective Holiday (videogame) 21–23
Deleuze, Gilles 24
Dérive 53–54, 89
Derrida 23, 52
digital nomadism 82–93
digital technology 17, 56
Diorama 1, 63
discovery 25, 32, 61
distance 2, 5, 009, 46, 61–62, 74, 90, 92–95, 98
dwelling 18–19

earth 92, 96, 99–100
ecology 19, 65
Elden Ring (videogame) 45–47
The Elder Scrolls IV: Oblivion (videogame) 63
emotions 20, 56, 60
environment 76, 90, 92, 98, 105

Index

Ergodic literature 31
Euro Truck Simulator 2 93–95
expansionism 8, 93
exploration 14, 16–17, 25, 40–41, 45, 57, 61, 63, 71, 75, 90–91

Firewatch 54–57
Flâneur 38–39
flow 19–21, 37–38, 44
Fortnite 18–19
Forza Horizon 5 (videogame) 91–93
Foucault, Michel 14
freedom 4, 15, 23, 37, 58, 60, 91, 96, 99
FS1 Flight Simulator (videogame) 96

Gadamer, Hans-Georg 24
Galloway, Alexander 24–25
gamification 17–19, 75, 82, 87
gazing 5, 8, 14, 31, 44, 53, 57, 65, 74, 92, 104
Gee, James Paul 23
Gibson, James 23
globalization 17
Goffman, Erving 62
Gone Home 53–54
Google Earth VR 99–100
GPS 87–88
Great Resignation 83
Grounded (videogame) 74–75

highways 93, 94, 97
home 8, 53–57, 76–77, 82, 95, 97–98
Homo Laborans 105
Howard, Todd 5, 74
Hyrule 1–2, 40, 43

imagination 5, 8, 14, 16, 31–33, 63, 71–75, 87, 98–99
immersion 16–18, 33, 35, 56, 88, 91
individualism 7, 36, 41, 56, 59, 95
internet 18, 92

Journey (videogame) 61–62

Kagen, Melissa 6, 25–26, 51, 54, 104

language of tourism 5
The Legend of Zelda (videogame) 1
The Legend of Zelda: Breath of the Wild (videogame) 2, 41
The Legend of Zelda: Ocarina of Time (videogame) 1–3, 40–45
The Legend of Zelda: Tears of the Kingdom (videogame) 102–3
location 8, 87, 90, 95, 99
locomotion 38, 61

MacCannell, Dean 62
masculinity 25, 38
Meta (company) 6, 18, 83, 101
metafiction 58
metaverse 6, 18–19, 77, 83, 100
Microsoft Flight Simulator 2020 (videogame) 95–99
Minecraft (videogame) 76–78
miniature 1, 62–63, 74
Miyamoto, Shigeru 1, 51–52
Miyazaki, Hidetaka 45
movement 17, 23, 32, 38, 52, 55, 61, 65, 87–88
Murray, Sean 71–73
myth 5, 8, 13–16, 58–60, 104–5

N64 Magazine 1–3
narrative 14, 16, 31–32, 54–58, 61–63, 91
nature 37, 41, 44, 53, 54, 72, 76, 78
Nintendo 2, 40, 41, 102
No Man's Sky (videogame) 70–73
non-places 94

optimization 17, 52
otherness 14, 105
Outer Wilds (videogame) 62–65
overview 4, 8, 36, 41–42, 45–47, 75, 96

The Path (videogame) 57
Percy, Walker 24
planet 41, 63–64, 72, 87, 90, 98–99
play 14, 20, 23–27, 51–52, 62, 65, 83, 90, 99
player-character 6
Pokémon Go (videogame) 87–90
polychronia 33

popularity 8, 19, 45, 76, 78, 80
postmodernity 58
procedural generation 59, 70–71, 73, 77
professionalism 93–94, 103
promontory gaze 37–41

remote work 81–83
Roblox (videogame) 18–19
romanticism 1, 17, 36–37, 40–41, 53

Salen, Katie 23
Sandbox games 32, 36, 38, 41
satellite 96, 99
Scale of game worlds 16, 32, 43–44, 52, 63–64, 71–75, 96, 103–4
Second Life (videogame) 18
semiotics 44, 52–53
Shklovsky, Viktor 26, 105
single-player 7, 102
size of game worlds 4, 40–41, 63, 71–73
social media 5, 18, 20, 60, 76–77
speedrunning 24
The Stanley Parable (videogame) 57–60
Stardew Valley (videogame) 78–79
Steam (video game platform) 23, 76, 99
Sterne, Lawrence 43
sublime 39–43, 63–65, 71–72, 75, 77
surrealists 53, 55–56
surveillance 14, 81, 90
survival games 70

theme parks 7, 33, 51
tourism 5–7, 13–14, 20, 23–24, 32–33, 36–38, 52–53, 57, 59, 62, 65, 76, 82, 88, 92
tourist gaze 8, 14, 22–23, 93, 103–5
travel 14–22, 44–46, 55–56, 64, 76, 82, 88, 94–95, 97–99

universe 56, 71–75, 79
urban 38, 76, 81–82, 89, 92
Urry, John 14
Utopia 92

virtuality 6, 18–19, 39
virtual reality (VR) 38–39, 99–100
virtual tourism 36, 92, 97–98
Visit Xbox 14–15

walking simulator 51–65
Wanderer above the Sea of Fog 3–4, 37, 42
wandering 25, 39, 61, 83
What Remains of Edith Finch (videogame) 54
work 13, 70, 80–83, 94–95, 103–4

You can go there 4–5, 8, 16, 23, 26, 46, 56, 58, 73–74, 99, 103
YouTube 24, 33, 76–77, 103

Zimmerman, Eric 23
Zork (videogame) 14

For Product Safety Concerns and Information please contact our EU representative GPSR@taylorandfrancis.com
Taylor & Francis Verlag GmbH, Kaufingerstraße 24, 80331 München, Germany

www.ingramcontent.com/pod-product-compliance
Lightning Source LLC
Chambersburg PA
CBHW051756230426
43670CB00012B/2310